1992

BEYOND PC

■ ■ ■ ■

TOWARD A POLITICS OF UNDERSTANDING

■ ■ ■

EDITED AND WITH AN
INTRODUCTION BY
PATRICIA AUFDERHEIDE

■ ■ ■ ■

Publication of this volume is made possible in part by a grant
provided by the Minnesota State Arts Board, through an appropriation
by the Minnesota State Legislature, and by a grant from the
National Endowment for the Arts. Additional support has been
provided by the Jerome Foundation, the Northwest Area Foundation,
and other generous contributions from foundations, corporations,
and individuals. Graywolf Press is a member agency of
United Arts, Saint Paul.

Published by Graywolf Press, 2402 University Avenue, Suite 203,
Saint Paul, Minnesota 55114. All rights reserved.
First Printing, 1992. Cover art: Mariii Lockwood, *Puzzle Piece*,
collection of Lanie and Tom Johnson.

9 8 7 6 5 4 3 2

Library of Congress Cataloguing-in-Publication Data
Beyond PC : toward a politics of understanding / edited and with an
introduction by Patricia Aufderheide.
p. cm.
ISBN 1-55597-164-4 (pbk.) : $10.00
1. Education, Higher—Political aspects—United States.
2. Education, Higher—Social aspects—United States.
3. Intercultural education—United States.   I. Aufderheide, Patricia.
LC89.B48   1992
370.19'341'0973—dc20   92-2513

ACKNOWLEDGMENTS

The essays collected in this anthology have appeared previously in publications, as noted below. We gratefully acknowledge the cooperation of editors, agents, and the authors for their permission to reprint the essays here.

Mortimer J. Adler's essay, appearing under the title "The Transcultural and the Multicultural," was published in a longer form in *The Great Ideas Today*, 1991. Copyright © 1991 by Encyclopaedia Britannica, Inc.

Molefi Kete Asante's statements, excerpted from "Multiculturalism: An Exchange," were published in *The American Scholar*, Spring 1991. Copyright © 1991 by the author. By permission of the publisher.

Katharine T. Bartlett's essay, appearing under the title "Some Factual Correctness about Political Correctness," was published in *The Wall Street Journal*, June 6, 1991. Copyright © 1991 by Katharine T. Bartlett.

David Beers's essay, appearing under the title "P.C.? B.S. : Behind the Hysteria: How the Right Invented Victims of PC Police," was published in a longer form in *Mother Jones*, September/October 1991. Copyright © 1991 by The Foundation for National Progress.

Paula Bennett's "Canons to the Right of Them . . ." was published in *The Women's Review of Books*, vol. VIII, no. 12, September 1991. Copyright © 1991 by Paula Bennett.

Michael Bérubé's statements, excerpted from "Public Image Limited—Political Correctness and the Media's Big Lie," were published in *The Village Voice*, June 18, 1991. Copyright © 1991 by Michael Bérubé.

Harry C. Boyte's essay, appearing under the title "Power and the Language of Difference: The Politics of Innocence," was published in *Liberal Education*, vol. 77, no. 1., January/February 1991. Copyright © 1991 by The Association of American Colleges, reprinted with permission.

Linda Brodkey and Shelli Fowler's essay, appearing under the title "Political Suspects," was published in *The Village Voice*, April 23, 1991. Copyright © 1991 by Linda Brodkey and Shelli Fowler.

George Bush's statements, excerpted from "Remarks at the University of Michigan Commencement Ceremony in Ann Arbor, May 4, 1991," were published in the *Weekly Compilation of Presidential Documents*, vol. 27, no. 19, May 13, 1991.

Reed Way Dasenbrock's "The Multicultural West" was published in *Dissent*, Fall 1991. Copyright © 1991 by *Dissent* and Reed Way Dasenbrock.

Sara Diamond's essay, appearing under the title "Readin', Writin', and Repressin'," was published in a longer form in *Z Magazine*, February 1991. Copyright © 1991 by Sara Diamond.

Dinesh D'Souza's "The Visigoths in Tweed" was published in *Forbes*, April 1, 1991. Copyright © 1991 by Dinesh D'Souza.

Martin Duberman's essay, appearing under the title "The Scholarship of Homosexuality," was published in *The Washington Post Education Review*,

April 7, 1991. Copyright © 1991 by *The Washington Post*, reprinted with permission.

Troy Duster's essay, appearing in a longer form under the title "They're Taking Over! And Other Myths about Race on Campus," was published in *Mother Jones*, September/ October 1991. Copyright © 1991 by The Foundation for National Progress.

Rosa Ehrenreich's "What Campus Radicals?" was published in *Harper's Magazine*, vol. 284, no. 1699, December 1991. Copyright © 1991 by *Harper's Magazine*.

Barbara Epstein's "'Political Correctness' and Identity Politics" was published in *Socialist Review*, December 1991. Copyright © 1991 by *Socialist Review*.

Sara M. Evans's essay, appearing under the title "Power and the Language of Difference: The Politics of Public Relations," was published in *Liberal Education*, vol. 77, no. 1., January/February 1991. Copyright © 1991 by The Association of American Colleges, reprinted with permission.

Elizabeth Fox-Genovese's statements, excerpted from "The Self-Interest of Multiculturalism," were published in *Tikkun*, vol. 6, no. 4, July/August 1991. Copyright © 1991 by *Tikkun*, a bimonthly Jewish critique of politics, culture, and society based in Oakland, CA.

Eugene D. Genovese's statements, excerpted from "Heresy, Yes—Sensitivity, No," were published in *The New Republic*, vol. 204, no. 15, April 15, 1991. Copyright © 1991 by *The New Republic*.

Todd Gitlin's "On the Virtues of a Loose Canon" was published in *New Perspectives Quarterly*, Summer 1991. Copyright © 1991 by *New Perspectives Quarterly*.

Miles Harvey's "Politically Correct Is Politically Suspect" was published in *In These Times*, December 25–January 14, 1991–92. Copyright © 1991 by Miles Harvey.

Eleanor Heartney's statements, excerpted from "The New Word Order," were published in *New Art Examiner*, April 1991. Copyright © 1991 by Eleanor Heartney.

Nat Hentoff's essay, appearing under the title "'Speech Codes' on the Campus and Problems of Free Speech," was published in *Dissent*, vol. 38, no. 4, Fall 1991. Copyright © 1991 by *Dissent* and Nat Hentoff.

Nina King's essay, appearing under the title "Classroom Notes: A Controversial English Department Deserves High Marks for Teaching," was published in *The Washington Post Education Review*, April 7, 1991. Copyright © 1991 by *The Washington Post*, reprinted with permission.

Louis Menand's statement, excerpted from "Illiberalisms," was published in *The New Yorker*, May 20, 1991. Copyright © 1991 by *The New Yorker*, reprinted with permission.

Raoul V. Mowatt's essay, appearing under the title "Stanford's Revolution That Wasn't Quite," was published in *The Washington Post Education Review*, April 7, 1991. Copyright © 1991 by *The Washington Post*, reprinted with permission.

National Association of Scholars, "The Wrong Way to Reduce Campus Tensions: A Statement of the National Association of Scholars," December 1991. Copyright © 1991 by The National Association of Scholars.

Ruth Perry's essay "A Short History of the Term Politically Correct" was published in a different form in *The Women's Review of Books*, February, 1992. Copyright © 1992 by Ruth Perry.

Diane Ravitch's statements, excerpted from "Multiculturalism: E Pluribus Plures," were published in *The American Scholar*, vol. 59, no. 3, Summer 1990. Copyright © 1990 by Diane Ravitch.

Joan Wallach Scott's essay, appearing under the title "The Campaign Against Political Correctness: What's Really at Stake?" was published in a longer form in *Change*, vol. 23, no. 6, November/December 1991. Copyright © 1991 by *Change*.

Teachers for a Democratic Culture's "Statement of Principles" was written by Gerald Graff, Gregory Jay, David Shumway, Jonathan Culler, Jane Gallop, and Houston Baker, 1991.

Michele Wallace's statement, excerpted from an interview with Michele Wallace by Jim Drobnick, was published in *Attitude: The Dancer's Magazine*. Copyright © 1991 by *Attitude: The Dancer's Magazine*.

Jacob Weisberg's "NAS – Who Are These Guys, Anyway?" was published in a longer form in *Lingua Franca: The Review of Academic Life*, vol. 1, no. 4, April 1991. Copyright © 1991 by *Lingua Franca: The Review of Academic Life*, published in New York.

Cornel West's statements, excerpted from "Diverse New World," were published in *Democratic Left*, July/August 1991. Copyright © 1991 by *Democratic Left*, a publication of Democratic Socialists of America.

Jon Wiener's "What Happened at Harvard" was published in *The Nation* magazine, September 30, 1991. Copyright © 1991 by *The Nation*.

Roger Wilkins's "A Modern Story" was published in *Mother Jones*, September/October 1991. Copyright © 1991 by The Foundation for National Progress.

George F. Will's "Literary Politics" was published in *Newsweek*, vol. CXVII, no. 16, April 22, 1991. Copyright © 1991 by Newsweek, Inc. All rights reserved. Reprinted by permission.

Patricia J. Williams's essay, appearing under the title "Blockbusting the Canon," was published in *Ms.*, September/October 1991. Copyright © 1991 by Patricia J. Williams.

Shawn Wong's essay, appearing under the title "The Asian-American Experience," was published in *The Washington Post Education Review*, April 7, 1991. Copyright © 1991 by *The Washington Post*, reprinted with permission.

C. Vann Woodward's "Freedom and the Universities" was published in a different form in *The New York Review of Books*, July 18, 1991. Reprinted with permission from *The New York Review of Books*. Copyright © 1991 Nyrev, Inc.

Contents

III. "IN MY EXPERIENCE..."

IV. BEYOND PC

V. MOSAIC

Introduction

■ ■ ■

PATRICIA AUFDERHEIDE

■ ■ ■

I T S O M E T I M E S S E E M S that more people are writing about "political correctness" than are actually experiencing it. Even the concept is slippery.

Is it a matter of whether you say "disabled" or "physically challenged"? Is the issue, as *Newsweek* charged in the December 1990 cover story that triggered the media onslaught about PC, "totalitarian" ways of teaching on American campuses? Or is it, as some in this anthology charge, largely a figment of the right-wing imagination, a strategy aimed at junking such programs as affirmative action? Is this debate about expanding the perimeters of the educational canon, or subverting the very notion of a canon – and, indeed, all intellectual standards?

PC; multiculturalism; the canon debate; deconstructionism and its discontents; bad manners and unisex bathrooms – there are moments when they all conflate in contrast to some good old days when people went to college to take Introduction to Knowledge and flunked if they couldn't punctuate. The accelerating cycle of pundits referencing other pundits has not clarified the terms of the debate.

But PC does have a reality beyond punditry, and so does the media-fed assault on PC, as the selections in this anthology show. This book explores the PC debate at the university level, with particular emphasis on teaching. This is because the assault on the PC phenomenon – shaping our very understanding of what it is – has come out of academe, with the formation of the National Association of Scholars (NAS). Out of liberal and left intellectual communities has come a diversity of responses to charges that PC is a danger to intellectual life in the academy.

The charges against political correctness, a range of which are excerpted in the first section, "Attack on PC," don't all come from the same political perspective. Perhaps the omnibus package is in Dinesh D'Souza's popular polemic, *Illiberal Education*, a synoptic sample of which is included here. Venerable American historian C. Vann Woodward finds his own experience echoed in D'Souza's book, as he explains here, and he takes seriously PC's threat to academic freedom. Other critics focus on particular aspects of this hydra-headed phenomenon. Nat Hentoff, always stern in defense of the First Amendment, denounces speech codes as a violation of freedom of expression. Mortimer Adler, in a stately recollection, presents a defense of great (not just good) books, and of truth rather than taste, displaying an enviable confidence in the unambiguousness of all those terms.

The denouncers of PC captured the media high ground early in the debate and secured their position with D'Souza's easy-reading best-seller. (Look in the short-excerpt final section, "Mosaic," for other morsels in the debate.) Much of the writing in response has had a defensive character, and also an invigorating reportorial air. "The Counterattack" showcases such responses, including Ruth Perry's history of the phrase. Several authors investigate the origins, background, and networks of the National Association of Scholars. Several more challenge the data on which some of the NAS's most serious charges are made. (These contributors range from participants in the PC battle, such as the teachers of the proposed English 306 at the University of Texas at Austin, to a *Washington Post* literary editor.) Finally, academic Katharine Bartlett succinctly employs Daphne Patai's concept of "surplus visibility" to explain why issues involving society's less powerful can become inflamed in the public imagination.

It has become common to counter charges of PCism by pointing to where the real power on campus is and how little ground it has ceded, as two students from elite universities do in "In My Experience . . . ." But how about the claim of Teachers for a Democratic Culture that "recent curricular reforms influenced by multiculturalism and feminism have greatly enriched education rather than corrupted it"? Authors Paula Bennett, Martin Duberman, Shawn Wong, and Roger Wilkins make the case — each in a very different way — for intellectual life that values cultural diversity. That doesn't mean, as Miles Harvey and Barbara Epstein note, that sanctimoniousness and self-righteousness aren't a problem in the university.

In fact, as Harry Boyte and Sara Evans make clear in their dialogue in "Beyond PC," sanctimony and powerlessness make a self-reinforcing match. For them, the problem is rooted in the paucity of public life in America today. By public life they mean a daily experience of resolving differences pragmatically. (Boyte's Project Public Life at the University of Minnesota's Hubert H. Humphrey Institute of Public Affairs offers a practical way to address the problem.) Berkeley's Troy Duster efficiently debunks myths about PCified campuses, and draws from students' ideas on how to turn the tensions of experiencing diversity into productive learning. As Duster argues, they're learning skills they'll need as citizens for the rest of their lives.

Other authors also offer visions beyond PC. Todd Gitlin describes the need to rescue ourselves from the "sound-bite culture" that consumerism has wrought, and calls for exit from disempowering identity politics to a politics of mutual respect. Reed Way Dasenbrock, who persuasively argues that the Western tradition is unavoidably multicultural, foresees the construction of a world culture. Patricia Williams calls for universities to create environments, both inside and beyond the classroom, where intercultural sensitivity can be cultivated and the notion of social equity can be entertained. Joan Scott describes a vision of community for the university in which difference is honored, respected, and turned back into a tool for shaping a shared space to work.

What is so impressive about this debate and the courageous,

creative responses it has evoked is the way it highlights the importance of the university in society. If the legacy of the PC debate is not to be a victory for procrustean curriculum reform, a ratification of the daily politics of fear and resentment, then we need these and other visions. In our polycultural democracy, we desperately need social spaces where we can differ productively, and the university is one of them.

I

ATTACK ON PC

■ ■ ■

The Wrong Way to Reduce Campus Tensions

■ ■ ■

THE NATIONAL ASSOCIATION OF SCHOLARS

■ ■ ■

THE ACADEMIC COMMUNITY *is alarmed by reports of intergroup tension at many colleges, including those long committed to equal opportunity. Unfortunately, educators have failed to reassess some recent policies and practices that, far from promoting tolerance and fairness, are undermining them. Worse yet, many have seized upon incidents of conflict to call for the extension of these policies and practices. They include:*

• A willingness to admit students widely disparate in their level of preparation in order to make the campus demographically representative

• Preferential hiring for faculty and staff positions determined by race, ethnicity, and gender

• Racially or ethnically exclusive financial aid and academic counseling programs, as well as special administrators, ombudsmen, and resource centers assigned to serve as the putative representatives of selected student groups

• Punitive codes restricting "insensitive" speech

• Mandatory "sensitivity training" for incoming freshmen and sometimes for all students, faculty, and staff

• Requirements that students take tendentious courses dealing with groups regarded as victimized

• A failure to enforce campus rules when violated by those promoting these policies or other "politically correct" causes.

*The National Association of Scholars believes that these policies
and practices involve either the application of a double standard or
the repudiation of appropriate intellectual criteria. Consequently,
they undercut the academy's special sense of common purpose and
prompt, divisive calculations of group interest. Specifically, we believe what follows.*

The admission of seriously underprepared students creates un-
realistic expectations and frequently leads to frustration and resentment. Moreover, policies that target specific minority groups
unfairly stigmatize all students in such groups, reinforcing negative stereotypes.

Two-track hiring threatens to produce a two-tiered faculty instead of a genuinely integrated one. While such hiring may well
create "role models," they will be the wrong kind, encouraging
the belief that it is the assertion of group power instead of the pursuit of individual achievement that reaps the most abundant
rewards.

Disadvantaged students deserve ample assistance, yet disad-
vantage need not coincide with race or ethnicity. Those excluded
are often frustrated by seeing individuals who may be no worse off
than themselves receiving special treatment solely because of ancestry. Furthermore, bureaucracies created to serve or champion
particular groups tend to have vested interests in emphasizing
differences, fostering complaints, and maintaining the separation
of those groups.

Safeguarding intellectual freedom is of critical importance to
the academy. Thus, it is deeply disturbing to see the concept of
"discriminatory harassment" stretched to cover the expression of
unapproved thoughts about selected groups or criticism of policies assumed to benefit them. Higher education should prepare
students to grapple with contrary or unpleasant ideas, not shield
them from their content. What is more, if a highly permissive attitude toward the excoriation of the "privileged" accompanies the
censorship of critical views about other groups, a backlash is pre-
dictable.

Tolerance is a core value of academic life, as is civility. College authorities should ensure that these values prevail. But tolerance involves a willingness, not to suppress, but to allow divergent opinions. Thus, "sensitivity training" programs designed to cultivate "correct thought" about complicated normative, social, and political issues do not teach tolerance but impose orthodoxy. And when these programs favor manipulative psychological techniques over honest discussion, they also undermine the intellectual purposes of higher education and anger those subjected to them.

If entire programs of study or required courses relentlessly pursue issues of "race, gender, and class" in preference to all other approaches to assessing the human condition, one can expect the increasing division of the campus along similar lines.

The discriminatory enforcement of campus regulations can only sap the legitimacy of academic authority and create a pervasive sense of mistrust. Indeed, should students feel that repeated violations not only go unpunished, but are actually appeased, the reckless may be tempted to take matters into their own hands. The final stage of discredit will be reached when students and faculty see in such appeasement attempts by administrators to justify their own programs of campus "reform."

The policies just described are generally well-intentioned. Nonetheless, if the goal were deliberately to aggravate campus tensions, the same policies might well be adopted. On the premise that the fair treatment of individuals can do as much to correct the current situation as the doctrine of collective guilt has done to create it, the National Association of Scholars urges the following:

• Admitting inadequately prepared students only when realistic provision can be made for remediation

• Maintaining nondiscriminatory hiring policies

• Eliminating all forms of institutional segregation and preferential treatment determined by race and ethnicity, together with administrative positions that foster ethnic dissension

• Protecting the expression of diverse opinion

• Avoiding programs that attempt to impose "politically correct" thinking

• Adding or retaining ethnic or gender studies courses only when they have genuine scholarly content and are not vehicles for political harangue or recruitment

• Enforcing campus rules, even with respect to those who feel they are violating them in a good cause.

The National Association of Scholars believes that the surest way to achieve educational opportunity for all and maintain a genuine sense of academic community is to evaluate each individual on the basis of personal achievement and promise. It is only as individuals united in the pursuit of knowledge that we can realize the ideal of a common intellectual life.

The Visigoths in Tweed

■ ■ ■

DINESH D'SOUZA

■ ■ ■

"I AM A MALE WASP who attended and succeeded at Choate (preparatory) School, Yale College, Yale Law School, and Princeton Graduate School. Slowly but surely, however, my life-long habit of looking, listening, feeling, and thinking as honestly as possible has led me to see that white, male-dominated, western European culture is the most destructive phenomenon in the known history of the planet.

"[This Western culture] is deeply hateful of life and committed to death; therefore, it is moving rapidly toward the destruction of itself and most other life forms on earth. And truly it deserves to die. . . . We have to face our own individual and collective responsibility for what is happening—our greed, brutality, indifference, militarism, racism, sexism, blindness. . . . Meanwhile, everything we have put into motion continues to endanger us more every day."

This bizarre outpouring, so reminiscent of the "confessions" from victims of Stalin's show trials, appeared in a letter to *Mother Jones* magazine and was written by a graduate of some of our finest schools. But the truth is that the speaker's anguish came not from any balanced assessment but as a consequence of exposure to the propaganda of the new barbarians who have captured the humanities, law, and social science departments of so many of our universities. It should come as no surprise that many sensitive young Americans reject the system that has nurtured them. At Duke University, according to the *Wall Street Journal*, professor Frank

Lentricchia in his English course shows the movie *The Godfather* to teach his students that organized crime is "a metaphor for American business as usual."

Yes, a student can still get an excellent education – among the best in the world – in computer technology and the hard sciences at American universities. But liberal arts students, including those attending Ivy League schools, are very likely to be exposed to an attempted brainwashing that deprecates Western learning and exalts a neo-Marxist ideology promoted in the name of multiculturalism. Even students who choose hard sciences must often take required courses in the humanities, where they are almost certain to be inundated with an anti-Western, anticapitalist view of the world.

Each year American society invests $160 billion in higher education, more per student than any nation in the world except Denmark. A full 45 percent of this money comes from the federal, state, and local governments. No one can say we are starving higher education. But what are we getting for our money, at least so far as the liberal arts are concerned?

A fair question? It might seem so, but in university circles it is considered impolite because it presumes that higher education must be accountable to the society that supports it. Many academics think of universities as intellectual enclaves, insulated from the vulgar capitalism of the larger culture.

Yet, since the academics constantly ask for more money, it seems hardly unreasonable to ask what they are doing with it. Honest answers are rarely forthcoming. The general public sometimes gets a whiff of what is going on – as when Stanford alters its core curriculum in the classics of Western civilization – but it knows very little of the systematic and comprehensive change sweeping higher education.

An academic and cultural revolution has overtaken most of our 3,535 colleges and universities. It's a revolution to which most Americans have paid little attention. It is a revolution imposed upon the students by a university elite, not one voted upon or even discussed by the society at large. It amounts, according to University of Wisconsin—Madison Chancellor Donna Shalala, to "a basic transformation of American higher education in the name of multiculturalism and diversity."

The central thrust of this "basic transformation" involves replacing traditional core curricula — consisting of the great works of Western culture — with curricula flavored by minority, female, and Third World authors.

Here's a sample of the viewpoint represented by the new curriculum. Becky Thompson, a sociology and women's studies professor, in a teaching manual distributed by the American Sociological Association, writes: "I begin my course with the basic feminist principle that in a racist, classist, and sexist society we have all swallowed oppressive ways of being, whether intentionally or not. Specifically, this means that it is not open to debate whether a white student is racist or a male student is sexist. He/she simply is."

Professors at several colleges who have resisted these regnant dogmas about race and gender have found themselves the object of denunciation and even university sanctions. Donald Kagan, dean of Yale College, says: "I was a student during the days of Joseph McCarthy, and there is less freedom now than there was then."

As in the McCarthy period, a particular group of activists has cowed the authorities and bent them to its will. After activists forcibly occupied his office, President Lattie Coor of the University of Vermont explained how he came to sign a sixteen-point agreement establishing, among other things, minority faculty hiring quotas. "When it became clear that the minority students with whom I had been discussing these issues wished to pursue negotiations *in the context of occupied offices* . . . I agreed to enter negotiations." As frequently happens in such cases, Coor's "negotiations" ended in a rapid capitulation by the university authorities.

At Harvard, historian Stephan Thernstrom was harangued by student activists and accused of insensitivity and bigotry. What was his crime? His course included a reading from the journals of slave owners, and his textbook gave a reasonable definition of affirmative action as "preferential treatment" for minorities. At the University of Michigan, renowned demographer Reynolds Farley was assailed in the college press for criticizing the excesses of Marcus Garvey and Malcolm X; yet the administration did not publicly come to his defense.

University leaders argue that the revolution suggested by these examples is necessary because young Americans must be taught to live in and govern a multiracial and multicultural society. Immigration from Asia and Latin America, combined with relatively high minority birth rates, is changing the complexion of America. Consequently, in the words of University of Michigan President James Duderstadt, universities must "create a model of how a more diverse and pluralistic community can work for our society."

No controversy, of course, about benign goals such as pluralism or diversity, but there is plenty of controversy about how these goals are being pursued. Although there is no longer a Western core curriculum at Mount Holyoke or Dartmouth, students at those schools must take a course in non-Western or Third World culture. Berkeley and the University of Wisconsin now insist that every undergraduate enroll in ethnic studies, making this virtually the only compulsory course at those schools.

If American students were truly exposed to the richest elements of other cultures, this could be a broadening and useful experience. A study of Chinese philosophers such as Confucius or Mencius would enrich students' understanding of how different peoples order their lives, thus giving a greater sense of purpose to their own. Most likely, a taste of Indian poetry such as Rabindranath Tagore's *Gitanjali* would increase the interest of materially minded young people in the domain of the spirit. An introduction to Middle Eastern history would prepare the leaders of tomorrow to deal with the mounting challenge of Islamic culture. It would profit students to study the rise of capitalism in the Far East.

But the claims of the academic multiculturalists are largely phony. They pay little attention to the Asian or Latin American classics. Rather, the non-Western or multicultural curriculum reflects a different agenda. At Stanford, for example, Homer, Plato, Dante, Machiavelli, and Locke are increasingly scarce. But often their replacements are not non-Western classics. Instead the students are offered exotic topics such as popular religion and healing in Peru, Rastafarian poetry, and Andean music.

What do students learn about the world from the books they are required to read under the new multicultural rubric? At Stanford one of the non-Western works assigned is *I, Rigoberta Menchú*, subtitled "An Indian Woman in Guatemala."

The book is hardly a non-Western classic. Published in 1983, *I, Rigoberta Menchú* is the story of a young woman who is said to be a representative voice of the indigenous peasantry. Representative of Guatemalan Indian culture? In fact, Rigoberta met the Venezuelan feminist to whom she narrates this story at a socialist conference in Paris, where, presumably, very few of the Third World's poor travel. Moreover, Rigoberta's political consciousness includes the adoption of such politically correct causes as feminism, homosexual rights, socialism, and Marxism. By the middle of the book she is discoursing on "bourgeois youths" and "Molotov cocktails," not the usual terminology of Indian peasants. One chapter is titled "Rigoberta Renounces Marriage and Motherhood," a norm that her tribe could not have adopted and survived.

If Rigoberta does not represent the convictions and aspirations of Guatemalan peasants, what is the source of her importance and appeal? The answer is that Rigoberta seems to provide independent Third World corroboration for Western left-wing passions and prejudices. She is a mouthpiece for a sophisticated neo-Marxist critique of Western society, all the more powerful because it seems to issue not from some embittered American academic but from a Third World native. For professors nourished on the political activism of the late 1960s and early 1970s, texts such as *I, Rigoberta Menchú* offer a welcome opportunity to attack capitalism and Western society in general in the name of teaching students about the developing world.

We learn in the introduction of *I, Rigoberta Menchú* that Rigoberta is a quadruple victim. As a person of color, she has suffered racism. As a woman, she has endured sexism. She lives in South America, which is—of course—a victim of North American colonialism. She is also an Indian, victimized by Latino culture within Latin America.

One of the most widely used textbooks in so-called multicultural courses is *Multi-Cultural Literacy*, published by Graywolf Press in St. Paul, Minnesota. The book ignores the *The Tale of Genji*, the Upanishads and Vedas, the Koran and Islamic commentaries. It also ignores such brilliant contemporary authors as Jorge Luis Borges, V.S. Naipaul, Octavio Paz, Naguib Mahfouz, and Wole Soyinka. Instead it offers thirteen essays of protest, including Michele Wallace's autobiographical "Invisibility Blues" and Paula Gunn Allen's "Who Is Your Mother? The Red Roots of White Feminism."

One student I spoke with at Duke University said he would not study *Paradise Lost* because John Milton was a Eurocentric white male sexist. At the University of Michigan, a young black woman who had converted to Islam refused to believe that the prophet Muhammad owned slaves and practiced polygamy. She said she had taken courses on cultural diversity and the courses hadn't taught her that.

One of the highlights of this debate on the American campus was a passionate statement delivered a few years ago by Stanford undergraduate William King, president of the Black Student Union, who argued the benefits of the new multicultural curriculum before the faculty senate of the university. Under the old system, he said, "I was never taught . . . the fact that Socrates, Herodotus, Pythagoras, and Solon studied in Egypt and acknowledged that much of their knowledge of astronomy, geometry, medicine, and building came from the African civilization in and around Egypt. [I was never taught] that the Hippocratic oath ac-

knowledges the Greeks' 'father of medicine,' Imhotep, a black
Egyptian pharaoh whom they called Aesculapius. . . . I was never
informed when it was found that the 'very dark and wooly haired'
Moors in Spain preserved, expanded, and reintroduced the classical knowledge that the Greeks had collected, which led to the
'renaissance.'. . . I read the Bible without knowing Saint Augustine looked black like me, that the Ten Commandments were almost direct copies from the 147 Negative Confessions of Egyptian
initiates. . . . I didn't learn Toussaint L'Ouverture's defeat of Na-
poleon in Haiti directly influenced the French Revolution, or that
the Iroquois Indians in America had a representative democracy
which served as a model for the American system."

This statement drew wild applause and was widely quoted. The
only trouble is that much of it is untrue. There is no evidence that
Socrates, Pythagoras, Herodotus, and Solon studied in Egypt, although Herodotus may have traveled there. Saint Augustine was
born in North Africa, but his skin color is unknown, and in any
case he could not have been mentioned in the Bible; he was born
over 350 years after Christ. Viewing King's speech at my request,
Bernard Lewis, an expert on Islamic and Middle Eastern culture
at Princeton, described it as "a few scraps of truth amidst a great
deal of nonsense."

Why does multicultural education, in practice, gravitate toward such myths and half-truths? To find out why, it is necessary
to explore the complex web of connections that the academic revolution generates among admissions policies, life on campus, and
the curriculum.

American universities typically begin with the premise that in
a democratic and increasingly diverse society the composition of
their classes should reflect the ethnic distribution of the general
population. Many schools officially seek "proportional representation," in which the percentage of applicants admitted from various racial groups roughly approximates the ratio of those groups
in society at large.

Thus universities routinely admit black, Hispanic, and American Indian candidates over better-qualified white and Asian American applicants. As a result of zealously pursued affirmative action programs, many selective colleges admit minority students who find it extremely difficult to meet demanding academic standards and to compete with the rest of the class. This fact is reflected in the dropout rates of blacks and Hispanics, which are more than 50 percent higher than those of whites and Asians. At Berkeley a study of students admitted on a preferential basis between 1978 and 1982 concluded that nearly 70 percent failed to graduate within five years.

For affirmative action students who stay on campus, a common strategy of dealing with the pressures of university life is to enroll in a distinctive minority organization. Among such organizations at Cornell University are Lesbian, Gay & Bisexual Coalition; La Asociacion Latina; National Society of Black Engineers; Society of Minority Hoteliers; Black Students United; and Simba Washanga.

Although the university brochures at Cornell and elsewhere continue to praise integration and close interaction among students from different backgrounds, the policies practiced at these schools actually encourage segregation. Stanford, for example, has "ethnic theme houses" such as the African house called Ujaama. And President Donald Kennedy has said that one of his educational objectives is to "support and strengthen ethnic theme houses." Such houses make it easier for some minority students to feel comfortable but help to create a kind of academic apartheid.

The University of Pennsylvania has funded a black yearbook, even though only 6 percent of the student body is black and all other groups appeared in the general yearbook. Vassar, Dartmouth, and the University of Illinois have allowed separate graduation activities and ceremonies for minority students. California State University at Sacramento has just established an official "college within a college" for blacks.

Overt racism is relatively rare at most campuses, yet minorities are told that bigotry operates in subtle forms such as baleful

looks, uncorrected stereotypes, and "institutional racism"—
defined as the underrepresentation of blacks and Hispanics
among university trustees, administrators, and faculty.

Other groups such as feminists and homosexuals typically get
into the game, claiming their own varieties of victim status. As
Harvard political scientist Harvey Mansfield bluntly puts it,
"White students must admit their guilt so that minority students
do not have to admit their incapacity."

Even though universities regularly accede to the political demands of victim groups, their appeasement gestures do not help
black and Hispanic students get a genuine liberal arts education.
They do the opposite, giving the apologists of the new academic
orthodoxy a convenient excuse when students admitted on a preferential basis fail to meet academic standards. At this point student activists and administrators often blame the curriculum.
They argue that it reflects a "white male perspective" that system-
atically depreciates the views and achievements of other cultures, minorities, women, and homosexuals.

With this argument, many minority students can now explain
why they had such a hard time with Milton in the English department, Publius in political science, and Heisenberg in physics.
Those men reflected white male aesthetics, philosophy, and science. Obviously, nonwhite students would fare much better if the
university created more black or Latino or Third World courses,
the argument goes. This epiphany leads to a spate of demands:
Abolish the Western classics, establish new departments such as
Afro-American Studies and Women's Studies, hire minority faculty to offer distinctive black and Hispanic "perspectives."

Multicultural or non-Western education on campus frequently
glamorizes Third World cultures and omits inconvenient facts
about them. In fact, several non-Western cultures are caste-
based or tribal, and often disregard norms of racial equality. In
many of them feminism is virtually nonexistent, as indicated by
such practices as dowries, widow-burning, and genital mutila-
tion; and homosexuality is sometimes regarded as a crime or men-

tal disorder requiring punishment. These nasty aspects of the non-Western cultures are rarely mentioned in the new courses. Indeed, Bernard Lewis of Princeton argues that while slavery and the subjugation of women have been practiced by all known civilizations, the West at least has an active and effective movement for the abolition of such evils.

Who is behind this academic revolution, this contrived multiculturalism? The new curriculum directly serves the purposes of a newly ascendant generation of young professors, weaned in the protest culture of the late 1960s and early 1970s. In a frank comment, Jay Parini, who teaches English at Middlebury College, writes, "After the Vietnam War, a lot of us didn't just crawl back into our library cubicles. We stepped into academic positions. . . . Now we have tenure, and the work of reshaping the university has begun in earnest."

The goal that Parini and others like him pursue is the transformation of the college classroom from a place of learning to a laboratory of indoctrination for social change. Not long ago most colleges required that students learn the basics of the physical sciences and mathematics, the rudiments of economics and finance, and the fundamental principles of American history and government. Studies by the National Endowment for the Humanities show that this coherence has disappeared from the curriculum. As a result, most universities are now graduating students who are scientifically and culturally impoverished, if not illiterate.

At the University of Pennsylvania, Houston Baker, one of the most prominent black academics in the country, denounces reading and writing as oppressive technologies and celebrates such examples of oral culture as the rap group N.W.A. (Niggers With Attitude). One of the group's songs is about the desirability of killing policemen. Alison Jaggar, who teaches women's studies at the University of Colorado, denounces the traditional nuclear family as a "cornerstone of women's oppression" and anticipates scientific advances enabling men to carry fetuses in their bodies so that child-bearing responsibilities can be shared between the sexes. Duke professor Eve Sedgwick's scholarship is devoted to unmasking what she terms the heterosexual bias in Western culture, a project that she pursues through papers such as "Jane Austen and the Masturbating Girl" and "How To Bring Your Kids Up Gay."

Confronted by racial tension and Balkanization on campus, university leaders usually announce that, because of a resurgence of bigotry, "more needs to be done." They press for redoubled preferential recruitment of minority students and faculty, funding for a new Third World or Afro-American center, mandatory sensitivity education for whites, and so on. The more the university leaders give in to the demands of minority activists, the more they encourage the very racism they are supposed to be fighting. Surveys indicate that most young people today hold fairly liberal attitudes toward race, evident in their strong support for the civil rights agenda and for interracial dating. However, these liberal attitudes are sorely tried by the demands of the new orthodoxy: many undergraduates are beginning to rebel against what they perceive as a culture of preferential treatment and double standards actively fostered by university policies.

Can there be a successful rolling back of this revolution, or at least of its excesses? One piece of good news is that blatant forms of racial preference are having an increasingly tough time in the courts, and this has implications for university admissions policies. The Department of Education is more vigilant than it used to be in investigating charges of discrimination against whites and Asian Americans. With help from Washington director Morton Halperin, the American Civil Liberties Union has taken a strong stand against campus censorship. Popular magazines such as *Newsweek* and *New York* have poked fun at "politically correct" speech. At Tufts University, undergraduates embarrassed the administration into backing down on censorship by putting up taped boundaries designating areas of the university to be "free speech zones," "limited speech zones," and "Twilight Zones."

Even some scholars on the political left are now speaking out against such dogmatism and excess. Eugene Genovese, a Marxist historian and one of the nation's most respected scholars of slavery, argues that "too often we find that education has given way to indoctrination. Good scholars are intimidated into silence, and the only diversity that obtains is a diversity of radical positions." More and more professors from across the political spectrum are resisting the politicization and lowering of standards. At Duke, for example, sixty professors, led by political scientist James David Barber, a liberal Democrat, have repudiated the extremism of the victims' revolution. To that end they have joined the National Association of Scholars, a Princeton, New Jersey–based group devoted to fairness, excellence, and rational debate in universities.

But these scholars need help. Resistance on campus to the academic revolution is outgunned and sorely needs outside reinforcements. Parents, alumni, corporations, foundations, and state legislators are generally not aware that they can be very effective in promoting reform. The best way to encourage reform is to communicate in no uncertain terms to university leadership and, if necessary, to use financial incentives to assure your voice is heard. University leaders do their best to keep outsiders from meddling or even finding out what exactly is going on behind the tall gates, but there is little doubt that they would pay keen attention to the views of the donors on whom they depend. By threatening to suspend donations if universities continue harmful policies, friends of liberal learning can do a lot. In the case of state-funded schools, citizens and parents can pressure elected representatives to ask questions and demand more accountability from the taxpayer-supported academics.

The illiberal revolution can be reversed only if the people who foot the bills stop being passive observers. Don't just write a check to your alma mater; that's an abrogation of responsibility. Keep abreast of what is going on and don't be afraid to raise your voice and even to close your wallet in protest. Our Western, free-market culture need not provide the rope to hang itself.

Literary Politics

■ ■ ■

GEORGE F. WILL

■ ■ ■

T HE MODERN Language Association's opposition to the
nomination of Carol Iannone to the National Council on the
Humanities is not quite sufficient reason for supporting her. But
MLA hostility is nearly necessary for creating confidence in anyone proposed for a position of cultural importance. The president
nominated Iannone at the behest of the chairman of the National
Endowment for the Humanities, Lynne Cheney, to whom the
council tenders advice. The MLA, composed mostly of professors
of literature and languages, is shocked—shocked!—that people
suspect it of political motives. Oh? The MLA is saturated with the
ideology that politics permeates everything. The unvarnished
truth is that the MLA's sniffy complaint amounts to this: Iannone
is not "one of us." Her writings confirm that virtue.

She teaches at NYU and is vice president of the National Association of Scholars, a burgeoning organization resisting the politicization of higher education. She is a trenchant critic of the
watery Marxism that has gone to earth in the MLA and elsewhere
on campuses. Academic Marxists deny the autonomy of culture,
explaining it as a "reflection" of other forces, thereby draining
culture of its dignity. The reduction of the study of literature to sociology, and of sociology to mere ideological assertion, has a central tenet: all literature is, whether writers are conscious of it or
not, political.

Writers, say the academics Iannone refutes, are captives of the
conditioning of their class, sex, race. All literature on which ca-

nonical status is conferred represents the disguised or unexamined assumptions and interests of the dominant class, sex, race. Hence culture is oppressive and a literary canon is an instrument of domination. This ideology radically devalues authors and elevates the ideologists – the critics – as indispensable decoders of literature, all of which is, by definition, irreducibly political.

Shakespeare's *Tempest* reflects the imperialist rape of the Third World. Emily Dickinson's poetic references to peas and flower buds are encoded messages of feminist rage, exulting clitoral masturbation to protest the prison of patriarchal sex roles. Jane Austen's supposed serenity masks boiling fury about male domination, expressed in the nastiness of minor characters who are "really" not minor. In *Wuthering Heights,* Emily Brontë, a subtle subversive, has Catherine bitten by a *male* bulldog. Melville's white whale? Probably a penis. Grab a harpoon!

The supplanting of aesthetic by political responses to literature makes literature primarily interesting as a mere index of who had power and whom the powerful victimized. For example, feminist literary criticism is presented as a political act, liberating women writers from the oppression of "patriarchal literary standards." Thus does criticism dovetail with the political agenda of victimology. The agenda is the proliferation of groups nursing grievances and demanding entitlements. The multiplication of grievances is (if radicals will pardon the expression) the core curriculum of universities that are transformed into political instruments. That curriculum aims at delegitimizing Western civilization by discrediting the books and ideas that gave birth to it.

Iannone tartly criticizes the "eruption of group politics in literature," noting that many scholarly activities, from the shaping of curricula to the bestowing of academic awards, have become instruments of racial, ethnic, and sexual reparations for Western civilization's sins. The Left's agenda does liberate, in this perverse way: it emancipates literature from the burden of aesthetic standards. All such standards are defined as merely sublimated assertions of power by society's dominant group. So all critics and authors from particular victim groups should be held only to the political standards of their group. Administration of these, and of the resulting racial and sexual spoils system in the academy, "requires" group politics: under the spreading chestnut tree, I tenure you and you tenure me.

As aesthetic judgments are politicized, political judgments are aestheticized: the striking of poses and the enjoyment of catharsis are central in the theater of victimization in academic life. All this, although infantile, is not trivial. By "deconstructing," or politically decoding, or otherwise attacking the meaning of literary works, critics strip literature of its authority. Criticism displaces literature and critics displace authors as bestowers of meaning.

It might seem odd, even quixotic, that today's tenured radicals have congregated in literature departments, where the practical consequences of theory are obscure. Obscure, but not negligible. As James Atlas writes, the transmission of the culture that unites, even defines America—transmission through knowledge of literature and history—is faltering. The result is collective amnesia and deculturation. That prefigures social disintegration, which is the political goal of the victim revolution that is sweeping campuses.

The fight over Iannone's nomination is particularly important precisely because you have not hitherto heard of it or her. The fight is paradigmatic of the many small skirmishes that rarely rise to public attention but cumulatively condition the nation's cultural, and then political, life. In this low-visibility, high-intensity war, Lynne Cheney is secretary of domestic defense. The foreign adversaries her husband, Dick, must keep at bay are less dangerous, in the long run, than the domestic forces with which she must deal. Those forces are fighting against the conservation of the common culture that is the nation's social cement. She, even more than a Supreme Court justice, deals with constitutional things. The real Constitution, which truly constitutes America, is the national mind as shaped by the intellectual legacy that gave rise to the Constitution and all the habits, mores, customs, and ideas that sustain it.

There has been a historic reversal: many of the most enlightened defenders of our cultural patrimony are now out in the "practical" world, including government, and many philistines are in the academies shaping tomorrow's elites, and hence tomorrow's governance. That is why Lynne Cheney and Carol Iannone matter more than do most of the things that get the public's attention.

Freedom and the Universities

■ ■ ■

C. VANN WOODWARD

■ ■ ■

DEFENDING FREEDOM under attack in universities invariably gets defenders into a variety of trouble. The attackers almost always profess devotion to free speech themselves—except when it is carried to extremes, or is used by fanatics to discredit a cause they believe to be of greater or nobler or more urgent importance, or when it gives offense or pain or distress to people with enough troubles already. Resort to one or another, if not several, of these exceptions will be made in almost any dispute over the limits of free speech. After all, it is only in such instances, at least as perceived by those who resort to these exceptions, that the issue of free speech is likely to arise.

Another embarrassment to champions of the free-speech principle is that they often share sympathy for the cause, the idea, or the oppressed minority presented as the exception to justify violations of the cherished principle. How can just causes be defended without injury to inviolable principle? The awkwardness can be increased when the advocate of free speech finds himself thrust into alliance with those who do not share his sympathies for the exceptional cause and urge freedom for quite different reasons. Under these circumstances the politics of academic freedom can become a bit complicated.

In a commencement address at the University of Michigan on

This edition of the essay is a revision by the author to correct such errors or misunderstandings of the original version as were revealed in the exchange following its publication and to add relevant information that became available later.

May 4, 1991, President Bush spoke out for freedom—freedom "to think and speak one's mind," perhaps "the most fundamental and deeply revered of all our liberties," yet one now under assault "on some college campuses." But two years earlier the President had proposed an amendment to the Bill of Rights against flag burning.

Dinesh D'Souza makes the word *politics* conspicuous in the title of his book *Illiberal Education: The Politics of Race and Sex on Campus*. His own political identifications have been and will undoubtedly be used to discredit his position on restriction of freedom and political abuses in the academy. D'Souza lines up on the right wing with a record of service to Reagan's White House, a fellowship in the American Enterprise Institute, early service on the unsavory *Dartmouth Review*, and later as a contributor to other journals on the Right. Yet his book comes with enthusiastic endorsements on the jacket by Eugene Genovese as well as Robert H. Bork and praise from all points across the political spectrum, along with censure from the *Village Voice*, the *Nation*, and others. Negative reviews stressing the author's politics seem to predominate and are sometimes used to dismiss his findings. But one need not be a right-winger to be concerned about the problems D'Souza raises, however welcome he may be as an ally.

One charge that cannot be used against the author of *Illiberal Education* is that he is a white Anglo-Saxon Protestant. He is in fact an immigrant from India with a secondary schooling in Bombay who did not arrive on these shores until 1978 and finds he "can still pass as a student." The vast religious, tribal, and cultural heterogeneity and conflict in his native land give him, he believes, "a unique cultural perspective" on present problems of ethnicity, race, and sex in the universities of his adopted country. While he leaves quite a different impression, he claims "a special kinship with minority students," especially their struggles for self-discovery, equality, and justice, "challenges I faced very recently in college and continue to face as a first-generation immigrant."

Announced politics and skin color of the author aside, what of the credibility and reliability of his book and its findings, and the importance of the subject addressed? An assessment of the subject's importance can better follow from the discussion below. As for accuracy of reporting and reliability of judgment, it would be wise to bear in mind that *Illiberal Education* is a polemical work written with strong conviction to condemn and to persuade, and that it is largely a collection of negative examples. Its moderation in tone and style may put readers off guard for its occasional stretching of evidence and logic to score a point. When I first wrote on the book I accepted its purely factual statements as true; on the whole, for a subject so heatedly debated up to the last moment, the investigation seemed reasonably thorough, the rhetoric comparatively temperate, and the documentation fairly detailed, if sometimes very selective. Unfortunately, the book turned out to contain some serious and irresponsible factual errors. Nevertheless, this was the most extensive critical study yet made of an academic convulsion that has been treated evasively or disingenuously by its administrators and with much more strident polemics by its activists. Agree with it or not, *Illiberal Education* appeared to deserve serious attention.

D'Souza writes six chapters on as many universities to illustrate and dramatize the radical changes in higher education in response to minority revolts. The universities are Berkeley, Stanford, Howard, Michigan, Duke, and Harvard. The problems exemplified are those of admissions and recruitment of students; curriculum and the assault on the "Dead White Male" Western canon; racial conflict, embitterment, and black withdrawal from campus integration; "sensitivity" and political indoctrination and censorship of opinion and expression—these along with problems of housing, budget, grading, and double standards. The author believes that while some of the worst aspects of the revolution occur in the six institutions chosen to illustrate the phenomena, their problems are widely experienced on other campuses, and he offers persuasive examples as evidence.

The most critical issue raised by the current academic upheaval is the denial of freedom—freedom of thought, speech, and teaching—academic freedom. It is critical because freedom is the very lifeline of universities, the indispensable condition of their being and mission. That issue has been at the center of every major attack on the academy of the last half century and more. To recall briefly only two recent ones, both beyond memory of the present generation, might supply a historical perspective missing in the account of the attack currently addressed and also indicate its distinctiveness.

The assault on academic freedom called McCarthyism began in the 1940s, before the senator from Wisconsin surfaced to become its symbol in the 1950s. The attack was nationwide and, while not confined to the academy, was extensively felt there in all respects. Careers were wrecked, scholars fled, institutes folded, journals collapsed, and books were censored, while the standards, values, and principles of higher education were subversively politicized. The most shameful thing was the frequency with which scholars under fire for their views and assertions were deserted by colleagues, administrators, and even the American Association of University Professors, their own defense organization. The oppression came from outside the university, had few active supporters within its walls, and was supported by Cold War activists in the government—federal, state, and local.

Unlike the assault on freedom in the fifties, that in the sixties came from within the academy, was led by students, supported by many professors, and justified on moral grounds to silence defenders of unpopular government policies, notably the Vietnam War. For some years speakers favoring disapproved views risked being shouted down, insulted, or even physically abused at some universities. Yale was not the worst, but on its campus a Nobel Laureate scholar, a governor, a U.S. secretary of state, and the U.S. commanding general were prevented from speaking. All of them took the unpopular side. That continued until the trustees, on the recommendation of the president and faculty, adopted a

code of university rules declaring a policy of "unfettered freedom" defined as "the right to think the unthinkable, discuss the
unmentionable, and challenge the unchallengeable." And as
cherished as civility and good fellowship are, the right of free
speech, offensive as it might become, must be assured priority.
Violations still occur at Yale, but miscreants face severe penalties and victims penalized for expressed opinions can appeal such
decisions successfully.

In the present crisis the attack on freedom comes from outside as
well as inside and is led by minorities, that is, people who speak
or claim to speak for groups of students and faculty. Their cause is
minority rights and sensitivities within the academy, instead of
change in national policies. In behalf of their cause and to protect
feelings from offensive speech they have, as we shall see, proved
themselves willing to silence speakers and professors, abuse
standards of scholarship, curriculum, and admissions, and impose conformity or silent submission on the campus. In these
strivings they have often received support from university admin-
istrations. Their greatest asset, however, is a moral one: the
demand for justice in behalf of groups that have long suffered in-
justice, discrimination, and deprivation. Some groups are larger
than others and some have suffered more than others, but all have
some claim on these grounds. Few would deny this. Another important asset is an ideological one: the very first of those truths in
the Declaration of Independence said "to be self-evident, that all
men are created equal" – to which Lincoln later said this nation
from the moment it was conceived was "dedicated."
   A perverse reading of the equality doctrine is frequently used
to justify the revolution in university recruitment and admission
of students. At Berkeley the new policy, in the name of "diversity," takes the form of seeking a student body that approximates
the proportions of blacks, Hispanics, whites, Asian Americans,
and other groups in California's population. Proportional admission was impossible to reconcile with old policies (not always

faithfully followed, to be sure) of acceptance according to merit and achievement, which would admit a disproportionately large percentage of high-scoring and rapidly increasing Asians and a very disproportionately low percentage of the black and Hispanic population. Chancellor Ira M. Heyman of Berkeley therefore resorted to what he called "a little social engineering." Merit criteria would be applied only *within* groups, accepting stronger over weaker blacks *and* Asians, but admitting much weaker black over superior Asian and white students. Thus some minorities gained by affirmative action and some lost. Some were treated as more equal than others. Whites, now a minority, were underrepresented in the entering class of 1989. Quotas intended to include also exclude. Speaking of achievement in social engineering, Vice Chancellor Roderic Parks boasted that "Berkeley has a bellwether role." Surely he did not intend one of the dictionary definitions of bellwether: "leader of a thoughtless crowd." But followers Berkeley did have.

The social engineers seem to have produced more problems than solutions. For one thing, they thrust affirmative action students, many of whom had not been given adequate preparation in elementary and high school, into situations in which they find it impossible to compete effectively at Berkeley. Thus fewer than 40 percent of blacks and fewer than 50 percent of Hispanics graduate. More than half drop out, about 30 percent of them before the end of their freshman year.

Highly selective as well as unselective universities continue to compete desperately in an ever-diminishing pool of talent for recruits of the proper skin color to fulfill some ideal of equality. There were indeed minority applicants with high qualifications and scores. Black scores in the Scholastic Aptitude Test for admission have improved slightly of late, but the overall white-black differential is still a huge 198 points in the aggregate, with only 116 out of 100,000 blacks who took the test in 1988 scoring over 699 out of 800 in the verbal section. As competition for qualified applicants sharpens, universities resort to inducements of high financial aid. An increasing number of universities restore subjective criteria and wave aside test scores.

As demand grew and supply diminished, more ill-equipped students were admitted and among them frustration, failures, and unhappiness multiplied. So did racial tensions, suspicions, slurs, and stereotypes. Defensive withdrawal and self-segregation were growing minority reactions, often with the encouragement and aid of university administrators eager to advance "pluralism" and "diversity." Minority dormitories, Third World clubs, African centers, and "ethnic theme houses" line some campuses to provide minority students havens from distress and anxieties bred in part by failures attributed to white bigotry and, in some cases, to incomprehensible reading assignments or lectures. Increasingly they have thought of themselves as groups rather than as individuals, and their culture as determined by their race.

One form separatism has taken is an attack upon the curriculum as an expression of white racial arrogance and propaganda, an attack accompanied by demands for a curriculum of their own. Compliant universities responded in the name of "multicultural" enrichment, diversity, and pluralism. Valid reasons did exist for complaint of outrageous curricular neglect and distortion in university curricula of minority contributions to Western civilization. But these reasons for complaint were used at times to denigrate and reject the whole heritage of Western civilization, the common culture to which they owed their very right to protest.

In a "message to the racist oppressors," quoted by D'Souza, the editor of a black student journal at Stanford framed his own protest by writing "we are tired of your shit." He was referring to a required course in the classics and history from the Greeks down. Jesse Jackson led a campus demonstration against the course on Martin Luther King Day in 1987, and a "Rainbow Coalition" of minority students and their supporters later occupied President Donald Kennedy's office. D'Souza describes how, despite the op-

position of the historian Carl Degler and a few others, in 1988 the
Stanford Faculty Senate voted 39 to 4 to drop the term *Western*
and substitute other requirements. So far D'Souza's account
seems accurate and has not been challenged so far as I know. His
account of the nature of changes in the Stanford curriculum, however, turns out to be seriously inaccurate. According to D'Souza
the university adopted a new course on American diversity required of all entering freshmen and described as "focusing on the
works of blacks, Hispanics, feminists, and homosexuals." Professor George Fredrickson of Stanford corrects this as follows:
"What was legislated was the requirement that students take one
course for one quarter at some point in their careers dealing with
racial, ethnic, and religious diversity in the United States. The
course may be chosen from a list of approximately twenty such
courses currently offered at Stanford."

Universities across the country followed Stanford's example,
with variations of their own. Some required a Third World or non-
Western course but made no requirement of a Western course.
D'Souza claims the text that "best reveals the premises underlying the new Stanford curriculum" is the study of *I, Rigoberta Menchú: An Indian Woman in Guatemala*. It is the transcription of an
oral autobiography. Whatever the shortcomings of this book as
literature, there proves to be nothing in it to justify D'Souza saying that she turned against European culture, renounced marriage and motherhood, and became a feminist and a Marxist.

It should be added that the philosopher John Searle, who also
deplored the tone of the campaign to change the Stanford curriculum, took a different view of the reforms themselves. He wrote
that seven of the eight different "tracks" of the required civilization courses from which students may choose

> are quite similar to the originals. To the required readings have
> been added such texts as Confucius, and the Koran, but I would
> guess that about 80 percent of the readings are by writers who are
> the same as, or comparable to, those in the previous program,

though the texts used are not exactly the same. If anything, these seven tracks look to me like a slight improvement on the original course in Western culture, because they retain enough of the core readings so that the educational purpose of the original is not lost, and at the same time they enrich course work with readings from outside the European tradition.

The new plan also offered members of the faculty the possibility of formulating a completely revised course and some teachers have done so, with the result that the eighth track is a course called "Europe and the Americas." In this course, the required elements of the European canon remain, but they are read along with works of Spanish-American, American-Indian, and African-American authors [including the work by Rigoberta Menchú discussed by D'Souza]. This eighth track presents a genuinely radical change from the earlier program, and it arouses the most objection.

However, it seems to me one can make a fairly strong case for the new course on purely educational grounds. Of eight tracks, it is not necessarily a bad thing to have one optional track where European civilization is taught as simply one civilization among others. [1]

Professor Searle believes that "coming to see one's own culture as one possible form of life and sensibility among others" can have a liberating effect. He is not upset by a reading list that includes Frantz Fanon along with Karl Marx and finds room for Aristotle and Tocqueville. On the whole he considers alarmist reports concerning the required freshman courses at Stanford "grossly exaggerated." "If I were a freshman at Stanford," he adds, "I might well be tempted to take 'Europe and the Americas.'"

Howard University is credited with producing more black professionals of distinction than any other university in the country and has wide influence at other black colleges. Its students militantly

1. John Searle, "The Storm over the University," *New York Review of Books*, December 6, 1990, p. 39.

advanced the cause of an Afrocentric curriculum. D'Souza finds that "the dominant political and academic enterprise of the students and faculty at Howard is aimed at discovering a cultural past that blacks can be proud of." To that end Howard's Department of African Studies and Research lists sixty-five courses, including numerous African language and dialect courses and others on the foreign policy, revolutions, and literature of African states and Islamic culture and philosophy. A separate Afro-American Studies Program adds twenty-five more courses, and the French department has a strong Afrocentric bent, for a university total of more than a hundred courses.

It is likely that some of the new Howard courses on African history, culture, and influence are legitimate and stimulating innovations. (It was little more than half a century ago that new courses in American history and culture struck Oxford and Cambridge as rather bizarre.) Side by side with African courses at Howard, courses of the older sort continue to be taught. But it is the Afrocentric studies that are still the most popular. Frank Snowden, professor of classics at Howard, is worried about misuse and distortion of ancient history and lore "to develop black pride." While that is understandable, Snowden says, he insists that "what we need is truth."

A new black scholarship relies heavily on appropriating achievements of ancient Egypt and claiming that Africa was schoolmaster to Greece and Rome. These ideas are currently popularized throughout the country and have become an article of faith among many black students at American universities and colleges. For scholarly authority they rely heavily on Martin Bernal, a Cornell professor of modern Chinese politics and his book, *Black Athena: The Afroasiatic Roots of Classical Civilization*. The purpose of his book, writes Bernal, is "to lessen European cultural arrogance" by arguments that Egyptian civilization was "fundamentally African," and that there were numerous "pharaohs whom one can usefully call black." However "useful" these claims or those for Egyptian origins of Greek and Roman

ideas may be for political purposes, they have certainly not convinced classical scholars.[2] Perhaps their vogue among blacks will
diminish with the realization that, as David Brion Davis points
out, in Egypt black slaves were "far more numerous than in the
Roman Empire," that Muslims began African slave trade one
thousand years before Europeans, and that Saudi Arabia did not
abolish slavery until the 1960s.[3] Or they may eventually recall
James Baldwin's words in *The Fire Next Time*: "The Negro has
been formed by this nation, for better or worse, and does not be-
long to any other—not to Africa, and certainly not to Islam."

Duke's plunge into the mainstream stressed star faculty appointments in several fields. It made a fine start by recruiting John
Hope Franklin, an outstanding historian whom I have often
praised for his lifelong refusal to permit his career, his scholarship, or himself to be segregated by race. Then things took a new
turn beginning in the spring of 1988 when a series of speakers, including Abbie Hoffman and Julian Bond, came on campus to
whip up protest among minority students and faculty, who demanded that all departments of the university appoint a "minority
professor." President Keith Brodie resisted on the ground that it
would be cynical to make promises that could not be kept in order
to gain favor, that qualified blacks were not available for all
fields, that compulsory hiring would result in appointees who
could not make tenure, and that no one stood to gain from lowered
standards. Three black faculty members joined with President
Brodie in the opposition, one saying there were not enough black
Ph.D.s in the sciences, and two on the ground that the appointments would place a stigma on all truly qualified black faculty.

2. For example, the review by Jasper Griffin, "Who Are These Coming to the
Sacrifice?" *New York Review of Books*, June 15, 1989; and Frank Turner, "Martin Bernal's *Black Athena*: A Dissent," in Molly Levine, editor, "The Challenge
of *Black Athena*," a symposium in the fall of 1989 issue of *Arethusa*.
3. David Brion Davis, *The Problem of Slavery in Western Culture* (Oxford University Press, 1966).

White faculty opposition on the Academic Council persisted. But there were more angry minority demonstrations. At one of them President Brodie appeared, apologized for his earlier remarks on lowered standards ("They sound foolish, which they were"), and surrendered. Next day the Academic Council switched their votes one by one and by 35 to 19 committed Duke to have at least one minority professor in each department by 1993. Not a racist school, Duke – not anymore.

That left several departments to find recruits who did not exist or were in very small numbers. Blacks receive only a little more than 2 percent of Ph.D. degrees; and about half of them are in education. The number has been declining – precipitously for black men. For numerous major fields there is a dearth of black doctorates and for some subjects scarcely any at all. In 1987 one was added in computer science, two in philosophy, three in chemical engineering and political science, four in mathematics and religion. In 1988 none was added in eight of the sciences, in European history, in classics, in comparative literature, or in the literature of five major countries. Under these handicaps and such feverish competition as characterized the hunt for black students, the mandated recruitment of minority faculty went forward with difficulty and it became stalled in places.

Four years before the commitment on compulsory minority faculty recruitment, Duke decided to recruit expensive superstars leading the then fashionable school of critics of the humanities who were known as deconstructionists. I am later assured by Clyde de L. Ryals of Duke that there is now "not one deconstructionist in the Duke English Department or in the Program in Literature." He goes on to say, however, "There are persons interested in gender, sexuality, Marxism, reader-reception, new-historicism, canonicity, popular culture, and many other types of criticism and theory . . . " This is no place to consider the brief and tormented history of deconstructionists and the belated revelations about one of their founding fathers. The question here is

what relation, if any, exists between their influence and the recruitment of minority faculty and the criteria of a multicultural
curriculum.

It seems safe to assume there was no intended connection and
that their coming together was more or less fortuitous. It is only
fair to concede that anything like full agreement on the tenets of
deconstruction theory is rare and that its followers do not claim in
any unified way to have a political view and that they have many
differences among them. That granted, it can be said that the burden of the movement's impact in some universities was a challenge to minimal standards of merit in faculty qualifications, and
the content and quality of what should be read and taught. Recur-
rent themes were the impossibility of objectivity, the futility of the
search for truth, and the absence of authority for designating any
works whatever as classics or part of a canon. The rhetoric of
some deconstructionists is carried to the point of trivializing the
idea of the humanities.[4]

The example of Duke in the construction of minority faculties
by compulsory goals was, with variations, followed by Wisconsin,
Purdue, Northern Illinois, Williams, Hampshire College, and
other eastern institutions. As competition for the extremely limited supply of minority teachers intensified, the quality of those
employed diminished and the salaries sometimes soared. "We
black scholars are enjoying our new marketability," a Duke professor who was soon to be lured to Harvard told D'Souza. Yet such
was the shortage of Ph.D.s that the number of full-time black faculty continued to decline. Courses in the name of "diversity"
tended to become more bizarre.

Departments in the natural sciences, mathematics, and engineering are less affected than others, and much teaching in the
social sciences and humanities goes on as before. Ethnocentric
programs and courses are often independent departments, and

4. David Lehman, *Signs of the Times: Deconstruction and the Fall of Paul de
Man* (Poseidon Press, 1991).

while some of them seek diversity to enrich a common national culture, a growing number insist that no culture is common or desirable to diverse Americans, and that one's culture is determined by one's race. The idea of a common culture is dismissed as white or Eurocentric propaganda.

Universities that were once centers of civil rights activists and advocates of racial integration are now reported not only by D'Souza but by colleagues who have written to me and to such organizations as the American Civil Liberties Union to be places where instances of bigotry are frequent. Anomalies multiply with the number of racial tensions, incidents, and conflicts. The more liberal the tradition and the more deference to protest, the more incidents are reported. Seemingly the more policies to promote harmony the greater the perception and complaint of racial hostility. Offenses are not exclusively from one race, but are perceived as racial only when the victim is from a minority group. However defined, by far the greater number of racial incidents occurs at northern universities, with those in Massachusetts leading them all. It is doubtful that the tide of withdrawal of minority groups into segregated dormitories, dining halls, student unions, clubs, fraternities, sororities, and even to an extent into separate curricula has promoted racial harmony. Yet university presidents have regularly welcomed, applauded, and financed such resegregations. President Harold Shapiro of Michigan (now president of Princeton) said that he could not grant all black professors tenure, but as demanded by Jesse Jackson, he agreed to give financial support to a new black student union and appropriated $27 million to increase minority faculty and student presence on campus.

Universities have thrived on controversy for centuries (when not asleep with orthodoxy and conformity), even when opposing sides were as sharply divided and intractable as in the present instance. Agreements sometimes emerged from gridlocked stalemate after vigorous debate when solutions seemed unavailable. But that has been possible only when both sides were free to have their say and speak their minds, even at the risk of being misunderstood, hurting causes they cherish, and bruising the feelings and sensibilities of friends. In the confrontation now at hand those essential freedoms are rapidly diminishing in many quarters and in some the ancient right of disputation has already yielded to the practice of indoctrination.

Curtailment or discouragement of free speech came, as often happens, to promote worthy moral causes. After some ugly slurs against blacks by white students, the University of Michigan developed more than a hundred programs of consciousness-raising and sensitivity-training for whites and plastered the campus with posters to protect minority feelings and stop white harassment and verbal attacks on blacks, including anonymously circulated statements recommending violence against them. When blacks held the programs themselves to be racist and white hostility continued, the next step was to adopt a code of racial etiquette and penalties for speech that violated it. Feminist and homosexual groups weighed in to add "sexist language" to the code of prohibitions. The policy adopted as punishable

> any behavior, verbal or physical, that stigmatizes or victimizes an
> individual on the basis of race, ethnicity, religion, sex, sexual ori-
> entation, creed, national origin, ancestry, age, marital status,
> handicap, or Vietnam-era veteran status.

Some faculty grumbled a bit about violations of classroom freedom, but most faculty and students acquiesced.

The only national organization to challenge Michigan's violation of the First Amendment was the American Civil Liberties Union. The ACLU filed a suit on behalf of an anonymous instructor in federal court, which struck down the entire Michigan policy as unconstitutional. U.S. District Judge Avern Cohn declared that "the Supreme Court has consistently held that states punishing speech or conduct solely on the grounds they are unseemly or offensive are unconstitutionally overbroad."

President James Ruderstat of Michigan had pronounced his university "a model of how a diverse and pluralistic community can work for society," and many institutions patterned their codes of speech control on that model. According to the *Chronicle of Higher Education,* policies restraining offensive language or conduct regarding race or sex have been adopted at Emory, Chapel Hill, Middlebury, Brown, Penn State, Tufts, and the Universities of California, Connecticut, Pennsylvania, and Wisconsin. Some of these codes, however, have been modified because of court decisions. Two professors at Stanford Law School urged censorship, one of them on the ground that the First Amendment had presupposed "the absence of societally created and culturally ingrained and internalized racism, sexism, and homophobia." Stanford adopted a rule restraining offensive speech in 1990, but as George Fredrickson has said, the restriction was limited to "a ban on verbal insults directed at an individual" and did not include other speech that might be considered offensive. Another lawyer pointed out with some irony that such rules and prohibitions were used a generation ago against students advocating racial equality and desegregation.

The Harvard program for propagating "sensitivity" includes several devices, one of which is AWARE week, an acronym for Actively Working Against Racism and Ethnocentrism. Organized by the assistant dean of minority affairs, it "designated race relations tutors" for each Harvard house, who were to report "violations," "monitor the racial atmosphere," and "raise consciousness." Harvard published an *Affirmative Action Newsletter* to expose myths such as one that affirmative action "means applying a double standard," which is denounced as "a proposition that is totally baseless."

To illustrate his impressions of restraints on academic freedom at Harvard, D'Souza makes much of the case of Professor Stephan Thernstrom in 1988, the unhappiness of three black students over certain statements of his in class, and the reactions of university administrators to the issues raised. Jon Wiener (see pp.

97-106) published findings that reveal how I and others were misled by D'Souza's account. For the administration's part in the matter, Dean of the College Fred Jewitt said that his statement on racial harrassment "had nothing to do with Thernstrom," Michael Spence, then Dean of the Faculty, said that he had praised the students as "judicious and fair" because they "avoided public comment" and not for criticizing Thernstrom. While Thernstrom felt Dean Spence had proved "sympathetic" and that there was never any threat of disciplinary action against him, he did feel that the administration might have been more supportive. In the end he stopped offering the course, but that was his decision and not the result of black agitation or administrative pressure.

A less publicized case arose in the Harvard Law School the following year. In 1989 a visiting law professor was attacked in an "open letter" by the head of the Harvard Women's Law Association for "promoting a dangerous misperception" because he quoted from Byron's *Don Juan* in his textbook. He defended himself at length, arguing that the quotation aptly illustrated a point of law. He said that if the Harvard Women's Law Association would supply "an equally concise, apt and literate quotation" that made the same point "without sex identification," he would use it in future revisions of his casebook. But he was attacked again in the Harvard Women's Law Association's newsletter. The administration remained silent and a few months later, according to D'Souza, Harvard released guidelines on "Sexism in the Classroom," saying "teachers should not focus attention on sex characteristics in a context in which sex would otherwise be irrelevant." The professor soon left Harvard, commenting that while some of his colleagues had made "private supportive gestures," the university was failing to recognize dangers to academic freedom.

Women and homosexuals do not receive nearly the proportion of attention suggested by the title of D'Souza's book. He does point out several relations, similarities, and differences between racial and sexual movements and their tendency to isolate their programs on the campus. Starting in 1970, women's studies has come to be a separate program or independent department in more than 500 American colleges and universities, while Afro-American studies has expanded from 78 programs in 1978 to about 350 now. One reason for this disparity is that many more qualified white female Ph.D.s than black Ph.D.s were available. Yet it is women who are seen to benefit from the momentum gained by black studies rather than vice versa. Professor Glenn Loury of Harvard complains that "feminists used the civil rights [race] issue to seize power in the universities" and to gain tenure and position. "Although we helped this to come about, yet we blacks have reaped very thin gains." Homosexuals as well as American Indians, Hispanics, and foreign students also gained attention for these complaints. Feminist extremists can hold their own with black extremists in competitive absurdities. For example, a professor at Washington University in St. Louis holds an "ovular" rather than a seminar, and one at McGill who refuses to use the adjective "seminal."

Among students and teachers identified with the majority, the response to minority demands and accusations of bigotry has been mixed and is of late in a state of transition. Responses to the appeal of sensitivity sessions to stand up and confess bigoted impulses and prejudices are not so forthcoming as they have been. A few years ago a Dartmouth student at such a meeting burst into tears as he confessed to being a homophobe, while fellow students sighed and applauded, and a Yale student had a seizure of repentance and remorse for his concealed racial biases. Of late, however, signs of boredom or sullenness have appeared among white students that threaten the coming of an ugly backlash and what D'Souza calls a "new racism." The old type of racism continues, but it was based on ignorance and is morally and politically discredited, whereas the new racism grows out of confrontation. The new racism, with its resentment of preferential treatment of blacks, often reinforces the old bigotry. A "White History Week" has appeared in reply to Black History Month. University-sponsored white student unions begin to turn up, and the protest from black student unions provokes amusement. The new racism is unrepentant and scornful of sensitivity indoctrination. Tactics developed to combat the old racism don't work against the new.

Another new racism has emerged among the minority groups, though it is not so identified by D'Souza. One of its effects is an awareness of administrative condescension that intensifies black insecurity. Whatever the public denials of a double standard, intelligent students can see what preferential treatment means, and they perceive the tacit administrative assumption of their inferiority, and the cynicism underlying it. It grows harder, in maintaining the status of victim and using the moral capital involved, to tell one's friends from one's flatterers. The flight from competition with better-prepared students in courses termed "white" to take refuge in black studies has not always proved satisfactory. Some students must have read the earlier warnings of Roy Wilkins, Kenneth Clark, and Bayard Rustin against "racial breast-beating," and Rustin's warning against using black studies "to escape the challenges of the university by setting up a program of 'soul courses' that they just play with and pass."

Others come to realize that the major works of black American scholars, including W.E.B. DuBois, Carter G. Woodson, and Alain L. Locke, were written before black studies departments came along. None of these three eminent scholars wanted their work isolated or their careers and fields of study determined by race. Yet John Hope Franklin, after pointing out that this was just what happened, writes:

> This was a tragedy. Negro scholarship had foundered on the rocks of racism. It had been devoured by principles of separation, of segregation. It had become the victim of the view that there was some "mystique" about Negro studies, similar to the view that there was some "mystique" about Negro spirituals which required that a person possess a black skin in order to sing them. This was not scholarship; it was folklore, it was voodoo.[5]

5. John Hope Franklin, *Race and History: Selected Essays, 1938–1988* (Louisiana State University Press, 1990).

Was it possible that the presumed beneficiaries of the new minority policies are really its victims, deprived of the liberal education they were promised, fed too often with political pablum, and graduated without preparation or deepened understanding and appreciation of the culture to which they were born and in which they are destined to live their lives?

One of the crueler ironies of the new racial policy of our universities is the stigma it has placed upon the black scholars of superior ability and intelligence who have honestly won high status and rank by their books and achievements. How often are the hard-won distinctions and honors they have gained smugly attributed to "affirmative action"? To cite a personal experience, I think of four former students who have gained admiration and praise for their books and won tenure in four of the most distinguished American universities. Not one of them has entirely escaped the assumption on the part of whites or blacks that all this is to be accounted for by the cynical politics of academic racial policy.

How are we to recover the humanism and understanding that are the goals of liberal education? How are our universities ever to pull out of the resegregation, the blatant tribalism, and competitive racial chauvinism they have inflicted upon themselves or permitted to grow and take over within their walls? How are they to encourage students not to substitute politics for learning? How can they weed out curricular nonsense, restore free speech, and revive standards? It will certainly not be easy. Genuine dilemmas and hard choices persist, conflicts between commitment to justice and commitment to intellectual integrity and quality. Administrators are hard pressed and have sometimes proved to be easily intimidated. D'Souza's "modest proposals" of nonracial affirmative action, no racial segregation, and a return to the classics, non-Western classics included, address long-range goals rather than immediate emergencies and measures.

For restoring or maintaining standards of scholarship it is natural to think of the associations with power to grant accreditation and to withhold or deny it to institutions that do not live up to standards. Loss of accreditation can be devastating. But the two associations with authority over middle Atlantic states and western states have recently announced that vigorous commitment to preferential recruitment of faculty, students, and multicultural curricula are essential criteria for accreditation. Not much help is to be expected from there. Nor from the American Association of University Professors. Then there are the national honorary societies such as Phi Beta Kappa, which extends membership only to those universities and colleges meeting scholarly standards. But, alas, some of the offenders are institutions with the highest scholarly prestige.

There remain the national associations of the scholarly disciplines, but some of those have fallen under leadership whose concerns are more political than scholarly, and a few, such as the Modern Language Association, are noted for clownish charades. The incoming president of the MLA, Houston Baker of the University of Pennsylvania, thinks "reading and writing are merely technologies of control" and considers "literacy" the menace. The MLA, however, has sponsored a national survey of university teachers of literature that finds a majority of the nearly 600 responding to their questions still cling to more or less traditional texts and methods.[6] Complaints nevertheless continue to pour in about misuse and political abuse of the curriculum and academic life.

Despair is common. A friend at Michigan State writes me that

> standard after standard has fallen. Every course must be gender-and-race related; chairs are awarded on the sole ground that the occupant would be a good "role model" for this or that constituency, etc. etc. So I keep to myself.

A Wesleyan professor, Jeremy Zwelling, published an open letter to President William M. Chase telling of hostile attacks by

6. *MLA Newsletter*, Winter 1991. pp. 12–14.

students in three recent courses that he taught. In one, members of his own faith accused him of assigning anti-Semitic readings from the Old Testament. In a second, women students "successfully sabotaged a seminar" with charges of "emotional rape" and "lethal misogyny." And a third course "almost collapsed" under abusive protests that he was racist and elitist. President Chase came immediately to his defense in April of 1991 with an appeal for "genuine freedom of speech" on the campus.

If salvation is forthcoming it must come from within the academy. And for those with wide and longtime acquaintanceship in its walls there is reason for hope. American universities retain much of their old stamina. Academics of integrity, courage, and conviction are still present in numbers around the country. Many come to mind. They are of varied ages, races, and political views. It is good to see Eleanor Holmes Norton of Georgetown Law School denouncing the new racial separatism as "exactly what we were fighting against – it is antithetical to what the civil rights movement was all about." It is reassuring to find Arthur Schlesinger deploring "the fragmentation of our culture into a quarrelsome spatter of enclaves, ghettos and tribes." (He discusses these questions in *The Disuniting of America*.)[7]

One of several at Harvard to speak out is David Riesman, who in retirement is saddened by "a kind of liberal closed-mindedness" in which "everybody is supposed to go along with the so-called virtuous position." At Duke forty-odd colleagues, black and white, support Professor James David Barber's declaration that "what's going on in universities now threatens everything that a university is supposed to be about. . . . Students' minds are supposed to be trained, not converted politically." And from Eugene Genovese at the University of Georgia in Atlanta, Georgia, comes a ringing denunciation of "the new wave of campus barbarism" and a strong call for "the defense of academic

7. Whittle Direct Books (Knoxville, Tennessee).

freedom . . . an all-out counterattack by a coalition that cuts across all the lines of politics, race, and gender. It is time to close ranks."

University presidents and administrators have generally distinguished themselves for their acquiescence, timidity, and silence rather than for courageous resistance in the face of campus anarchy, violence, and barbarism. Fortunately there are a few exceptions, and one is President Benno C. Schmidt, Jr., of Yale. In a public address in New York on March 20, 1991,[8] he spoke out against the present "flabbiness of the tradition of liberal education," deplored "an institution that doubts its fundamental purpose," and any university leadership "that is queasy about defending academic values." As an authority on the First Amendment, he regretted the "pall of conformity on many campuses" and "the complacency with which many are responding." His own response was anything but complacent. He firmly reiterated the rule of "unfettered freedom" on his own campus, and continued: "Some of the finest universities in this country have adopted rules which empower groups of faculty and students with roving commissions to punish offensive speech." When this happens, he concluded, "a lethal and utterly open-ended engine of censorship is loosed." Its greatest damage is not to those punished, but to "the vastly greater number of speakers who will steer clear of possible punishment," and the "chilling effects of vague powers to punish offensive speech."

With support of this sort for freedom and sanity from academics of learning and influence, there is reason for hope that the current aberration in the academy may be halted before it is too late. It would be easy to add to those already mentioned many names of scholars who would also rally to the defense of free speech. What is needed is that they too stand up, be counted, and speak out. The time for this has indeed come.

8. Excerpts were published in *The Wall Street Journal* on May 6, 1991.

"Speech Codes" and Free Speech

■ ■ ■

NAT HENTOFF

■ ■ ■

DURING THREE YEARS of reporting on anti-free-speech tendencies in higher education, I've been at more than twenty colleges and universities – from Washington and Lee and Columbia to Mesa State in Colorado and Stanford.

On this voyage of initially reverse expectations – with liberals fiercely advocating censorship of "offensive" speech and conservatives merrily taking the moral high ground as champions of free expression – the most dismaying moment of revelation took place at Stanford.

In the course of a two-year debate on whether Stanford, like many other universities, should have a speech code punishing language that might wound minorities, women, and gays, a letter appeared in the *Stanford Daily*. Signed by the African-American Law Students Association, the Asian-American Law Students Association, and the Jewish Law Students Association, the letter called for a harsh code. It reflected the letter and the spirit of an earlier declaration by Canetta Ivy, a black leader of student government at Stanford during the period of the grand debate. "We don't put as many restrictions on freedom of speech," she said, "as we should."

Reading the letter by this rare ecumenical body of law students (so pressing was the situation that even Jews were allowed in), I thought of twenty, thirty years from now. From so bright a cadre of graduates, from so prestigious a law school would come some of the law professors, civic leaders, college presidents, and maybe even a Supreme Court justice of the future. And many of them would have learned—like so many other university students in the land—that censorship is okay provided your motives are okay.

The debate at Stanford ended when the president, Donald Kennedy, following the prevailing winds, surrendered his previous position that once you start telling people what they can't say, you will end up telling them what they can't think. Stanford now has a speech code.

This is not to say that these gags on speech—every one of them so overboard and vague that a student can violate a code without knowing he or she has done so—are invariably imposed by student demand. At most colleges, it is the administration that sets up the code. Because there have been racist or sexist or homophobic taunts, anonymous notes or graffiti, the administration feels it must *do something*. The cheapest, quickest way to demonstrate that it cares is to appear to suppress racist, sexist, homophobic speech.

Usually, the leading opposition among the faculty consists of conservatives—when there is opposition. An exception at Stanford was law professor Gerald Gunther, arguably the nation's leading authority on constitutional law. But Gunther did not have much support among other faculty members, conservative or liberal.

At the University of Buffalo Law School, which has a code restricting speech, I could find just one faculty member who was against it. A liberal, he spoke only on condition that I not use his name. He did not want to be categorized as a racist.

On another campus, a political science professor for whom I had great respect after meeting and talking with him years ago has been silent—students told me—on what Justice William Brennan once called "the pall of orthodoxy" that has fallen on his campus.

When I talked to him, the professor said, "It doesn't happen in my class. There's no 'politically correct' orthodoxy here. It may happen in other places at this university, but I don't know about that." He said no more.

One of the myths about the rise of PC is that, coming from the Left, it is primarily intimidating conservatives on campus. Quite the contrary. At almost every college I've been to, conservative students have their own newspaper, usually quite lively and fired by a muckraking glee at exposing "politically correct" follies on campus.

By and large, those most intimidated—not so much by the speech codes themselves but by the Madame Defarge-like spirit behind them—are liberal students and those who can be called politically moderate.

I've talked to many of them, and they no longer get involved in class discussions where their views would go against the grain of PC righteousness. Many, for instance, have questions about certain kinds of affirmative action. They are not partisans of Jesse Helms or David Duke, but they wonder whether progeny of middle-class black families should get scholarship preference. Others have a question about abortion. Most are not pro-life, but they believe that fathers should have a say in whether the fetus should be sent off into eternity.

Jeff Shesol, a recent graduate of Brown, and now a Rhodes scholar at Oxford, became nationally known while at Brown because of his comic strip, *Thatch*, which, not too kindly, parodied PC students. At a forum on free speech at Brown before he left, Shesol said he wished he could tell the new students at Brown to have no fear of speaking freely. But he couldn't tell them that, he said, advising the new students to stay clear of talking critically about affirmative action or abortion, among other things, in public.

At that forum, Shesol told me, he said that those members of the Left who regard dissent from their views as racist and sexist should realize that they are discrediting their goals. "They're honorable goals," said Shesol, "and I agree with them. I'm against racism and sexism. But these people's tactics are obscuring the goals. And they've resulted in Brown no longer being an open-minded place." There were hisses from the audience.

Students at New York University Law School have also told me that they censor themselves in class. The kind of chilling atmosphere they describe was exemplified last year as a case assigned for a moot court competition became subject to denunciation when a sizable number of law students said it was too "offensive" and would hurt the feelings of gay and lesbian students. The case concerned a divorced father's attempt to gain custody of his children on the grounds that their mother had become a lesbian. It was against PC to represent the father.

Although some of the faculty responded by insisting that you learn to be a lawyer by dealing with all kinds of cases, including those you personally find offensive, other faculty members supported the rebellious students, praising them for their sensitivity. There was little public opposition from the other students to the attempt to suppress the case. A leading dissenter was a member of the conservative Federalist Society.

What is PC to white students is not necessarily PC to black students. Most of the latter did not get involved in the NYU protest, but throughout the country many black students do support speech codes. A vigorous exception was a black Harvard Law School student who spoke during a debate on whether the law school should start punishing speech. A white student got up and said that the codes are necessary because, without them, black students would be driven away from colleges and thereby deprived of the equal opportunity to get an education.

The black student rose and said that the white student had a hell of a nerve to assume that he—in the face of racist speech—would pack up his books and go home. He'd been familiar with that kind of speech all his life, and he had never felt the need to run away from it. He'd handled it before and he could again.

The black student then looked at his white colleague and said that it was condescending to say that blacks have to be "protected" from racist speech. "It is more racist and insulting," he emphasized, "to say that to me than to call me a nigger."

But that would appear to be a minority view among black students. Most are convinced they do need to be protected from wounding language. On the other hand, a good many black student organizations on campus do not feel that Jews have to be protected from wounding language.

Though it's not much written about in reports of the language wars on campuses, there is a strong strain of anti-Semitism among some — not all, by any means — black students. They invite such speakers as Louis Farrakhan, the former Stokely Carmichael (now Kwame Touré), and such lesser but still burning bushes as Steve Cokely, the Chicago commentator who has declared that Jewish doctors inject the AIDS virus into black babies. That distinguished leader was invited to speak at the University of Michigan.

The black student organization at Columbia University brought to the campus Dr. Khallid Abdul Muhammad. He began his address by saying: "My leader, my teacher, my guide is the honorable Louis Farrakhan. I thought that should be said at Columbia Jewniveristy."

Many Jewish students have not censored themselves in reacting to this form of political correctness among some blacks. A Columbia student, Rachel Stoll, wrote a letter to the *Columbia Spectator*: "I have an idea. As a white Jewish American, I'll just stand in the middle of a circle comprising. . . Khallid Abdul Muhammad and assorted members of the Black Students Organization and let them all hurl large stones at me. From recent events and statements made on this campus, I gather this will be a good cheap method of making these people feel good."

At UCLA, a black student magazine printed an article indicating there is considerable truth to the *Protocols of the Elders of Zion*. For months, the black faculty, when asked their reactions, preferred not to comment. One of them did say that the black students already considered the black faculty to be insufficiently militant, and the professors didn't want to make the gap any wider. Like white liberal faculty members on other campuses, they want to be liked—or at least not too disliked.

Along with quiet white liberal faculty members, most black professors have not opposed the speech codes. But unlike the white liberals, many honestly do believe that minority students have to be insulated from barbed language. They do not believe—as I have found out in a number of conversations—that an essential part of an education is to learn to demystify language, to strip it of its ability to demonize and stigmatize you. They do not believe that the way to deal with bigoted language is to answer it with more and better language of your own. This seems very elementary to me, but not to the defenders, black and white, of the speech codes.

Consider University of California president David Gardner. He has imposed a speech code on all the campuses in his university system. Students are to be punished—and this is characteristic of the other codes around the country—if they use "fighting words"—derogatory references to "race, sex, sexual orientation, or disability."

The term *fighting words* comes from a 1942 Supreme Court decision, *Chaplinsky* v. *New Hampshire*, which ruled that "fighting words" are not protected by the First Amendment. That decision, however, has been in disuse at the High Court for many years. But it is thriving on college campuses.

In the California code, a word becomes "fighting" if it is directly addressed to "any ordinary person" (presumably, extraordinary people are above all this). These are the kinds of words that are "inherently likely to provoke a violent reaction, *whether or not they actually do*." (Emphasis added.)

Moreover, he or she who fires a fighting word at any ordinary person can be reprimanded or dismissed from the university because the perpetrator should "reasonably know" that what he or she has said will interfere with the "victim's ability to pursue effectively his or her education or otherwise participate fully in university programs and activities."

Asked Gary Murikami, chairman of the Gay and Lesbian Association at the University of California, Berkeley: "What does it mean?"

Among those — faculty, law professors, college administrators -- who insist such codes are essential to the university's purpose of making *all* students feel at home and thereby able to concentrate on their work, there has been a celebratory resort to the Fourteenth Amendment.

That amendment guarantees "equal protection of the laws" to all, and that means to all students on campus. Accordingly, when the First Amendment rights of those engaging in offensive speech clash with the equality rights of their targets under the Fourteenth Amendment, the First Amendment must give way.

This is the thesis, by the way, of John Powell, legal director of the American Civil Liberties Union (ACLU), even though that organization has now formally opposed all college speech codes — after a considerable civil war among and within its affiliates.

The battle of the amendments continues, and when harsher codes are called for at some campuses, you can expect the Fourteen Amendment — which was not intended to censor *speech* — will rise again.

A precedent has been set at, of all places, colleges and universities, that the principle of free speech is merely situational. As college administrators change, so will the extent of free speech on campus. And invariably, permissible speech will become more and more narrowly defined. Once speech can be limited in such subjective ways, more and more expression will be included in what is forbidden.

One of the exceedingly few college presidents who speaks out on the consequences of the anti-free-speech movement is Yale University's Benno Schmidt:

> Freedom of thought must be Yale's central commitment. It is not easy to embrace. It is, indeed, the effort of a lifetime. . . . Much expression that is free may deserve our contempt. We may well be moved to exercise our own freedom to counter it or to ignore it. But

universities cannot censor or suppress speech, no matter how ob-
noxious in content, without violating their justification for existence. . . .

On some other campuses in this country, values of civility and
community have been offered by some as paramount values of the
university, even to the extent of superseding freedom of expression.

Such a view is wrong in principle and, if extended, is disastrous to freedom of thought. . . . The chilling effects on speech of
the vagueness and open-ended nature of many universities'
prohibitions . . . are compounded by the fact that these codes are
typically enforced by faculty and students who commonly assert
that vague notions of community are more important to the academy than freedom of thought and expression. . . .

This is a flabby and uncertain time for freedom in the United
States.

On the Public Broadcasting System in June 1991, I was part of
a Fred Friendly panel at Stanford University in a debate on
speech codes versus freedom of expression. The three black pan-
elists, including a Stanford student, strongly supported the
codes. So did the one Asian American on the panel. But then so
did Stanford law professor Thomas Grey, who wrote the Stanford
code, and Stanford president Donald Kennedy, who first opposed
and then embraced the code. We have a new ecumenicism of
those who would control speech for the greater good. It is hardly a
new idea, but the mix of advocates is rather new.

But there are other voices. In the national board debate at the
ACLU on college speech codes, the first speaker – and I think
she had a lot to do with making the final vote against codes un-
animous – was Gwen Thomas. A black community college administrator from Colorado, she is a fiercely persistent exposer of
racial discrimination.

She started by saying, "I have always felt as a minority person
that we have to protect the rights of all because if we infringe on
the rights of any persons, we'll be next.

"As for providing a nonintimidating educational environment, our young people have to learn to grow up on college campuses. We have to teach them how to deal with adversarial situations. They have to learn how to survive offensive speech they find wounding and hurtful."

Gwen Thomas is an educator — an endangered species in higher education.

Multiculturalism, Transculturalism, and the Great Books

■ ■ ■

MORTIMER J. ADLER

■ ■ ■

THE CONTROVERSY ABOUT multiculturalism at the college level focuses on the books that should be a part of one's general education. It is a dispute about the traditionally recognized canon of the monuments of Western literature in all fields – works of mathematics and science as well as works of poetry, drama, and fiction, and also works of biography, history, philosophy, and theology. Here we are confronted with current attacks upon the canonical list of great books and the responses that those attacks have elicited.

I am involved in this controversy – as associate editor of the first edition of the *Great Books of the Western World,* published in 1952, and as editor in chief of the second, much expanded edition, published in 1990.

The second edition differed from the first in many respects: new translations, a revised *Synopticon,* and six volumes of twentieth-century authors that did not appear in the first edition, as well as fifteen authors added in the period from Homer to Freud. As in the case of the first edition, so in the case of the second: our editorial board and the large group of advisers we consulted did not agree unanimously about the authors to be included; but in both cases there was 90-percent agreement. That, in my judgement, is all one can expect in a matter of this kind.

I would like to call attention to two things about the second edition. In writing an introductory essay, which appeared in a volume that accompanied the set titled *The Great Conversation*, I anticipated the controversy that the second edition of the *Great Books of the Western World* would arouse. This did not arise before. In the 1940s, when we were engaged in producing the first edition, *Eurocentric* was not current as a disapprobative term. There was no hue and cry about the absence of female authors; nor had blacks cried out for representation in the canon. In those earlier decades of this century, students and teachers in our colleges and educators in general were not concerned with multiculturalism in our educational offerings.

The second edition contains female authors, some in the nineteenth and some in the twentieth century, but no black authors; and it is still exclusively Western (i.e., European or American authors) with none from the four or five cultural traditions of the Far East.

The controversy over the desirability of multiculturalism having arisen in the late 1980s, I took account of it in my introductory essay, pointing out carefully the criteria in terms of which the authors were selected for inclusion, explaining the difference between the 500 or so *great* works included in the set and the thousands of *good* books listed in the recommended readings at the end of each of the 102 chapters in the *Synopticon*. These lists included many female and many black authors, but none from the Far East.

These exclusions were not, and are not, invidious. The difference between *great* and *good* books is one of kind, not of degree. Good books are not "almost great" or "less than great" books. Great books are relevant to human problems in every century, not just germane to current twentieth-century problems. A great book requires reading over and over, and has many meanings; a good book need be read no more than once, and need have no more than one meaning.

I also explained but did not apologize for the so-called Eurocentrism of the *Great Books of the Western World* by pointing out why no authors or works from the four of five distinct cultural traditions in the Far East were included or should be included. The Western authors are engaged in a great conversation across the centuries about great ideas and issues. In the multicultural traditions of the Far East, there are, perhaps, as many as four or five great conversations about different sets of ideas, but the authors and books in these different cultural traditions do not combine these ideas in one Far Eastern tradition, nor do they participate in the great conversation that has occurred over the last twenty-five centuries in the West. There are undoubtedly great, as distinguished from good, books in all of these Far Eastern traditions.

I did not anticipate the nature of the response to the publication of the second edition by those who challenged its Eurocentrism or who complained about the fact that its authors were still for the most part dead white males, with few females and no blacks. They based their challenges on press announcements of the list of included authors, but without reading my introductory essay and without knowing that a large number of female and black authors were included in the 102 lists in the *Synopticon* of *good* books cited as readings recommended in addition to the great books included in the set, along with many other books by white males, none of them regarded as great.

I should mention one other point that is highly germane to the controversy. Many of those who criticize the traditional canon of great books and call for its rejection incorrectly suppose that its defenders claim that it is a repository of transcultural truth and nothing else. That is not the case. The editors and advisory consultants of the *Great Books of the Western World* know that there is much more error or falsity in the intellectual and cultural tradition of the West than there is truth.

The relation of truth to error is a one-to-many ratio; for every truth, there are many deviations from it that are false. What truth is to be found is, of course, transcultural. The multiple errors, some of them multicultural, that impinge on each truth are of great importance for the understanding of the truth. Without grappling with the errors, one's understanding of the truth that corrects them is shallow. It follows that if the truths to be found in the great books of the West are transcultural, so, too, must be the understanding of the errors, some of which will be discovered in the Far East.

I turn now from the controversy about the second edition of the *Great Books of the Western World* to the controversy that has very recently arisen concerning what books should be required reading in colleges that still have some interest in the general, as opposed to the specialized, education of their students. This controversy started at Stanford University in 1988 and has spread since then to other colleges across the country.

The popular press and the electronic media have given the controversy ample notice, and its pros and cons have been publicly debated. A desirable multiculturalism has been appealed to as the basis not only for including many recent books by female, black, and non-Western authors but also for eliminating from the required readings a large number of authors and books that have long been treasured as Western greats, especially authors and books in classical antiquity, in the Middle Ages, and in modern times up to the nineteenth century.

Unquestionably among the books that have been recommended for addition, some contain recently discovered or restated truths that correct errors to be found in books of earlier centuries. If so, who could reasonably object to such additions? No one. But the same cannot be said for the recommended deletions from the list of required readings — Plato and Aristotle, for example; Herodotus, Thucydides, and Gibbon; Homer, Virgil, Dante, Shakespeare, and Tolstoy; Marcus Aurelius, Rabelais, Montaigne, Hobbes, Locke, Rousseau, and John Stuart Mill. All of these dead white males made important contributions to the pursuit of truth, even if there was much error in their insights, their principles, or their conclusions. Why, then, should many of them, or any of them, be rejected, if their inclusion does not call for the rejection of twentieth-century books written by female or black authors?

If general education is to include not just Western civilization but the other great cultures of the world in the Far East, a question still remains. If Western civilization is included as one of many in the multicultural mélange, why exclude Western authors and books long recognized as truly great for their contribution to the pursuit and understanding of truth?

It may be said, of course, that there is not enough time to include these older authors if twentieth-century authors and Far Eastern authors are also to be added to the required readings. It may be said that general education should be given up and no readings at all should be required for that purpose.

But it should not be said, as some of the proponents of multiculturalism seem to think, that truth is merely what some people assert. And that they would like to be the ones to assert what is true, or to elect those who are to assert it. Or if objective truth is held to exist somewhere, it is in natural science, but not in speculative philosophy, theology, or religion, and especially not in moral philosophy, which is concerned with questions of value—good and evil, right and wrong, what ought to be sought and done.

For such multiculturalists, these are all held to be matters of subjective personal predilection. They are not matters of public knowledge, not even knowledge with residual doubt, but only private or individual opinion, unsupported by the weight of evidence or reasons. What is or is not desirable is, therefore, entirely a matter of taste (about which there should be no disputing), not a matter of truth that can be disputed in terms of empirical evidence and reasons.

That being the case, we are left with a question that should be embarrassing to the multiculturalists, though they are not likely to feel its pinch. When they proclaim the desirability of the multicultural, they dispute about matters that should not be disputed. What, then, can possibly be their grounds of preference? Since in their terms it cannot appeal to any relevant body of truth, what they demand in the name of multiculturalism must arise from a wish for power or self-esteem.

When dispute on a basis of empirical evidence or by appeal to rational grounds is ruled out, conflicting claims can only be resolved by power politics, either by force or by dominance of a majority. In either case, it comes down to might makes right. That is exactly what is happening today in the efforts of the multiculturalists to change the curriculum in the public schools and in our colleges.

Multiculturalism is cultural pluralism. In the twentieth century, pluralism has become part of the democratic ideal, opposed to the monolithic totalitarianism that is now being challenged in the Soviet Union, and also to the equally monolithic rigidity of Islamic, Jewish, or Christian fundamentalism.

While democracy and socialism, and with them pluralism, are ideal in the social and economic dimensions of society, cultural pluralism is not wholly desirable in other dimensions of our life. What is desirable is a *restricted* cultural pluralism; that is, the promotion and preservation of pluralism in all matters of taste, but not in any matters that are concerned with objectively valid truth, either descriptive factual truth or prescriptive normative truth.

In this century, mathematics, the hard-core natural sciences, and their attendant technologies have become transcultural. What truth they have so far attained is at present acknowledged everywhere on earth. Whether or not in the next century or in a more distant future transcultural truth will be attained in philosophy, in the social sciences, in institutional history, and even in religion is an open question that should not be dogmatically answered by the present breed of multiculturalists whose unrestricted pluralism substitutes power or might for truth and right in the effort to control what should be taught or thought.

II

THE COUNTERATTACK

Statement of Principles

■ ■ ■

TEACHERS FOR A
DEMOCRATIC CULTURE

■ ■ ■

COLLEGES AND UNIVERSITIES in the United States have lately begun to serve the majority of Americans better than ever before. Whereas a few short years ago institutions of higher education were exclusive citadels often closed to women, minorities, and the disadvantaged, today efforts are being made to give a far richer diversity of Americans access to a college education. Reforms in the content of the curriculum have also begun to make our classrooms more representative of our nation's diverse peoples and beliefs and to provide a more truthful account of our history and cultural heritage. Much remains to be done, but we can be proud of the progress of democratization in higher education.

A vociferous band of critics has arisen, however, who decry these changes and seek to reverse them. These critics have painted an alarming picture of the state of contemporary education as a catastrophic collapse. This picture rests on a number of false claims: that the classics of Western civilization are being eliminated from the curriculum in order to make race, gender, or political affiliation the sole measure of a text's or subject's worthiness to be taught; that teachers across the land are being silenced and politically intimidated; that the very concepts of reason, truth, and artistic standards are being subverted in favor of a crude ideological agenda. It is our view that recent curricular reforms influenced by multiculturalism and feminism have greatly enriched education rather than corrupted it. It is our view as well that the controversies that have been provoked over admissions and hiring practices, the social functions of teaching and scholarship, and the status of such concepts as objectivity and ideology are signs of educational health, not decline.

Contrary to media reports, it is the National Association of Scholars, their corporate foundation supporters, and like-minded writers in the press who are endangering education with a campaign of harassment and misrepresentation. Largely ignorant of the academic work they attack (often not even claiming to have read it), these critics make no distinction between extremists among their opposition and those who are raising legitimate questions about the relations of culture and society. And though these critics loudly invoke the values of rational debate and open discussion, they present the current debate over education not as a legitimate conflict in which reasonable disagreement is possible, but as a simple choice between civilization and barbarism.

Yet because the mainstream media have reported misinformed opinions as if they were established facts, the picture the public has received of recent academic developments has come almost entirely from the most strident detractors of these developments. These inaccurate accounts, moreover, appear in forums that rarely invite the accused parties to present their side of the story. As Michael Bérubé has pointed out, "Recent literary theory is so rarely accorded the privilege of representing itself in nonacademic forums that journalists, disgruntled professors, embittered ex-graduate students, and their families and friends now feel entitled to say anything at all about the academy without fear of contradiction by general readers. The field is wide open, and there's no penalty for charlatanism (quite the contrary), since few general readers are informed enough to spot even the grossest forms of misrepresentation and fraud."

There is blatant hypocrisy, furthermore, when the charge of politicizing the humanities comes from right-wing ideologues. Dinesh D'Souza, the author of the widely discussed and excerpted *Illiberal Education*, is a former domestic policy analyst of the

Reagan administration, a research fellow at the conservative American Enterprise Institute, and a founding editor of the notorious *Dartmouth Review,* which received a $150,000 grant from the Olin Foundation in 1991. Current National Endowment for the Humanities (NEH) Chair Lynne V. Cheney boasts of being a "conservative populist" even as she excoriates her critics for politicizing education.

These contradictions were seen in the recent debate over the nomination of Carol Iannone to the National Council on the Humanities. In the wake of Iannone's defeat, Cheney and others have now predictably blamed the outcome on the intolerant forces of "political correctness." But it is Cheney who has proved herself consistently intolerant of any view of scholarship that does not agree with her own. What has gone unnoticed in the commentary on the Iannone case is the growing ideological one-sidedness of the National Council. In disregard of the "comprehensive representation" of scholarly and professional views explicitly mandated by Congressional legislation, the council has been packed with such appointees as National Association of Scholars members Peter Shaw and Edwin J. Delattre and outspoken conservatives like Donald Kagan. As Richard Cohen wrote in the *Washington Post,* "Had Iannone written brilliantly in defense of feminism. . . , Cheney would have looked elsewhere." Since the council oversees NEH grant applications, purging it of a diversity of viewpoints makes it possible to deny grants to scholars who take the wrong political line in their work.

It is time for those who believe in the values of democratic education and reasoned dialogue to join together in an organization that can fight such powerful forms of intolerance and answer mischievous misrepresentations. We support the right of scholars and teachers to raise questions about the relations of culture, scholarship, and education to politics — not in order to shut down debate on such issues but to open it. It is just such a debate that is prevented by discussion-stopping slogans like "political correctness."

What does the notion of a "democratic culture" mean and how

does it relate to education? In our view, a democratic culture is one that acknowledges that criteria of value in art are not permanently fixed by tradition and authority, but are subject to constant revision. It is a culture in which terms like *canon, literature, tradition, artistic value, common culture,* and even *truth* are seen as disputed rather than given. This means not that standards for judging art and scholarship must be discarded, but that such standards should evolve out of democratic processes in which they can be thoughtfully challenged.

We understand the problems in any organization claiming to speak for a very diverse, heterogeneous group of teachers who may sharply disagree on many issues, including that of the politics of culture. What we envision is a coalition of very different individuals and groups, drawn from many academic disciplines, bound together by the belief that recent attacks on new forms of scholarship and teaching must be answered in a spirit of principled discussion. The very formation of such a group will constitute an important step in gaining influence over the public representations of us and our work.

It will also be a way to take responsibility for the task of clarifying our ideas and practices to the wider public – something, clearly, we have not done as well as we should. We need an organization that can not only refute malicious distortions, but also educate the interested public about matters that still remain shrouded in mystery – new theories and movements, such as deconstruction, feminism, multiculturalism, and the new historicism, and their actual effects in classroom practice.

A Short History of the Term
Politically Correct

■ ■ ■

RUTH PERRY

■ ■ ■

T HE PHRASE *politically correct*, like a will-o'-the-wisp on
the murky path of history, has glimmered and vanished
again as successive movements for social change have stumbled
across the uncertain terrain. Its erratic appearance has always
brought consternation as well as relief, resistance as well as con-
sent. Like a recurring refrain in a song, or an incantatory line in a
poem, its meaning changes each time it appears.

The phrase seems first to have gained currency in the U.S. in
the mid to late 1960s within the Black Power movement and the
New Left, although the phenomenon—labeling certain acts and
attitudes as right or wrong—must be as old as belief itself.[1] Indeed, anthropologists will tell you that all communities evolve
group norms about behavior and ideology. But in the era in which
politically correct emerged as a popular phrase, the various
groups that made use of it were all newly organized, whistling in
the dark, trying to get their bearings, reaching for common terms
to name the *plastic, corporate, mechanistic, alienated, white-
supremacist, sexist, militaristic* society they wanted to change.

Feminists of various stripes, Black Panthers, activists against
the Vietnam War or against the House Un-American Activities

---

1. In a recent letter to the *Chronicle of Higher Education* (June 26, 1991),
Howard M. Ziff writes that he remembers the phrase used in the early 1950s as a
euphemism for "party line"; but I have found no corroboration of this usage from
historians of the Old Left, card-carrying members, or longtime associates.

Committee, civil rights workers, Muslims and other elements of
the Black Power movement, hippies, and countercultural paci-
fists – all of these groups were evolving their own agendas, their
own internal dynamics, their own organizing strategies, their own
political tactics, their own identities. Officially suspicious of the
older generation (Question authority! Don't trust anyone over
thirty!), these groups saw themselves as discontinuous with past
movements: fresh, new, and visionary.

In this context, the phrase *politically correct* meant as many
different things as the people who used it. Usually marked with
quotation marks or italics, it expressed a combination of distrust
for party lines of any kind and a simultaneous commitment to
whichever dimension of social change that person was working
for. Used every which way – straight, ironically, satirically, in-
terrogatively – it focused and expressed all the uncertainties
about dogmatism and preachiness that these new movements
were questioning, including the pieties of the Old Left, of corporate America, and of the government.

It probably came into the New Left vocabulary through translations of Mao Tse-tung's writings, especially in "the little red
book" as it was known, *Quotations from Chairman Mao Tse-tung*.
Mao used the word *correct* a lot (or rather his translators used it),
as in "correct" or "incorrect" ideas. In a speech from 1957, "On
the Correct Handling of Contradictions Among the People," first
translated in 1966 and widely disseminated in excerpts in the little red book, he stated that "the only way to settle questions of an
ideological nature or controversial issues among the people is by
the democratic method, the method of discussion, of criticism, of
persuasion and education, and not by the method of coercion or
repression."[2] This is the same essay in which he advocated "letting a hundred flowers blossom" and "letting a hundred schools of

2. *Quotations from Chairman Mao Tse-Tung* (Peking: Foreign Languages
Press, 1966), 52. Mao did not, of course, invent the concept of "correct" ideas.
As far back as 1935, Joseph Wood Krutch, in an article called "On Academic
Freedom" published in the *Nation* (April 17, 1935), noted that leftists were be-
ginning to sound more like conservatives in believing that "'correct' opinions,"
as opposed to debate and conflicting ideas, should be taught in school.

thought contend" and "long term co-existence and mutual super-vision." In other words, the Maoist position at the time was that correct thinking — thinking that would help the new socialist state survive — could be achieved by free speech, contention, and mutual criticism. These three conditions of thought and speech were assumed to entail one another rather than to inhibit one another.

The little red book had an enormous influence on the New Left because it was read avidly by two constituencies, by black as well as by white radicals. The Black Panthers sold it to raise money. Black revolutionaries from the cultural nationalists to the Muslim pan-Africanists quoted it. In fact the earliest memories of the term *politically correct* that I have been able to elicit from friends and acquaintances on either the New or the Old Left, are the memories of black friends guilt-tripping or being guilt-tripped about their dedication to the Black Power movement. To be politically incorrect in the late sixties as a black was to be an Uncle Tom, a nonrevolutionary, or a sloppy person — a hippie, for instance. Going with a white person was definitely incorrect. Women who stood up to their black brothers as feminists rather than staying within traditional nurturing female roles were also incorrect.

Indeed, the earliest textual reference to the phrase that I have found is in an essay by Toni Cade (not, as yet, Bambara), "On the Issue of Roles," in the anthology she edited in 1970, *The Black Woman*. In the essay she tells a teaching anecdote about confronting gender prejudice in a black class by reading aloud an antifeminist paper in which all the references to men and women had been changed to "us" and "them," thus disguising the sexism as racism. "And sure enough everyone reacted to phrases like 'I don't believe in the double standard, but' or 'They're trying to take over' and agreed it was the usual racist shit." When the uproar died down after she revealed her trick, the point remained, as she put it: "Racism and chauvinism are anti-people. And a man cannot be politically correct and a chauvinist too."[3]

3. This essay was excerpted from a lecture delivered to the Livingston College Black Women's Seminar in 1969.

The next year, 1971, Toni Cade Bambara published a book for children, *Tales and Stories for Black Folks*. In the contributors' notes she described herself as a "young Black woman who writes, teaches, organizes, lectures, tries to learn and tries to raise her daughter to be a correct little sister." Within months, Audre Lorde responded to this with a poem with a very long title: "Dear Toni/ Instead of a Letter of Congratulation/ Upon your Book And Your Daughter/ Whom You Say You Are Raising To Be/ A Correct Little Sister."

Audre Lorde's poem takes issue with Bambara's boast about raising her daughter to be correct, and claims experience as the only training for "correctness":

> I know beyond fear and history
> that our teaching means keeping trust
> with less and less correctness
> only with ourselves —

For this poet, no less dedicated to the struggle for black women, the notion of political correctness stuck in her craw. Still she was grateful to her friend and sister Toni Cade for "going and becoming/ the lessons you teach your daughter," for her warrior spirit, and for her commitment. She ends the poem hopefully, blessing both their daughters, and pointing out that she and Toni Cade together form the landscape for these girls:

> printed upon them as surely
> as water etches feather on stone.
> Our girls will grow into their own
> Black Women
> finding their own contradictions
> that they will come to love
> as I love you.

Do not lose sight of the personal in the political, she is saying. Our daughters will become who they are in relation to who we are; they will have their own battles to fight, their own contradictions to handle.

Almost from the start, then, the phrase occasioned a dispute over what defined "politically correct" and over its uncritical use. That accords with Maurice Isserman's memory about the use of the phrase in the early seventies, recently recorded in an article in *Tikkun*. "It was always used in a tone mocking the pieties of our own insular political counterculture," he wrote, "as in 'We *could* stop at McDonald's down the road if you're hungry,' or 'We *could* spend good money to get the television fixed,' etc. – 'but it wouldn't be politically correct.'"[4]

There were some, no doubt, like the young Toni Cade, who used the phrase straight up, without irony, without self-mockery. But almost as soon as anyone did use it that way, it was picked up and parodied by the skeptics, the anarchists, the individualists – whoever was worrying about the constraints of dogma.

This history was repeated with a vengeance in the so-called Sex Wars, the debates among feminists about women's sexuality, about pornography, and especially about lesbian sadomasochistic practices. Positions in the Sex Wars polarized at the famous Barnard College conference "The Scholar and the Feminist IX: Towards a Politics of Sexuality," held April 24, 1982. One of the purposes of this conference was to question whether there was such a thing as "politically correct" sexual practice, and to address issues of pleasure and fear, "acknowledging that sexuality is simultaneously a domain of restriction, repression, and danger, as well as a domain of exploration, pleasure, and agency."[5] From the earliest stages of planning for this conference, in September 1981, the question of "political correctness" had come up, in quotes, in relation to female sexuality. Muriel Dimen proposed to examine the "links between sexual 'political correctness' and other forms of 'political correctness' both on the Left and the

4. Maurice Isserman, "Travels with Dinesh," *Tikkun*, vol. 6, no. 5, 1991: 82.
5. This "Concept Paper" was published as an addendum to *Pleasure and Danger*, ed. Carole S. Vance (Boston and London: Routledge and Kegan Paul, 1984), 443–46.

Right."[6] What was a feminist to do if her sexual gratification was tied to "politically incorrect" fantasies? Were antipornography activists simply re-inscribing Victorian images of prudish "good girls"? Was the "prosex" faction simply enacting patriarchal paradigms of domination and submission and playing into the hands of a billion-dollar pornography industry that exploited and dehumanized women?

The conflict was exacerbated by a "Speakout on Politically Incorrect Sex" sponsored by the Lesbian Sex Mafia, many of whom were, according to Ann Ferguson, "self-identified 'S/M' lesbian feminists who argue that the moralism of the radical feminists stigmatizes sexual minorities such as butch/femme couples, sadomasochists, and man/boy lovers, thereby legitimizing 'vanilla sex' lesbians and at the same time encouraging a return of a narrow, conservative, 'feminine' vision of ideal sexuality."[7] The speakout was, in turn, picketed by the Coalition for a Feminist Sexuality and against Sadomasochism, whose leaflet protested the exclusion from the conference of "feminists who have developed the feminist analysis of sexual violence, who have organized a mass movement against pornography, who have fought media images that legitimize sexual violence, who believe that sadomasochism is reactionary, patriarchal sexuality, and who have worked to end the sexual abuse of children."[8]

Each side felt that the other side was standing in the way of liberation; each felt that the other was working against the interests of women. The so-called radical feminists accused the Lesbian Sex Mafia of politically incorrect sexual practices, and the LSM

6. Hannah Alderfer et al., eds., *Diary of a Conference on Sexuality* (New York: Faculty Press, 1982). A searching essay on the subject by Muriel Dimen was subsequently published in Carole S. Vance, ed. *Pleasure and Danger*, 138–48.
7. Ann Ferguson et al., "Forum: The Feminist Sexuality Debates," *Signs*, vol. 10, no. 1 (1984): 107. Ann Ferguson's introduction to this fascinating collection of position papers on the subject is beautifully documented. See also Carla Freccero, "Notes of a Post-Sex Wars Theorizer," in *Conflicts in Feminism*, ed. Marianne Hirsch and Evelyn Fox Keller (New York and London: Routledge, 1991): 305–25.
8. The entire leaflet is reprinted in *Feminist Studies*, vol. 9, no. 1 (Spring 1983): 180–82.

in turn gleefully appropriated this terminology and began to flaunt it as enviable, sexy, radical. Within lesbian circles, being "politically incorrect," like being a "bad girl," was coming to mean hip, sophisticated, rebellious, impulsive.

Meanwhile, the organizers of the Barnard conference and their supporters circulated and published a letter deploring the censoriousness of such groups as Women Against Pornography and Women Against Violence Against Women. "Feminist discussion about sexuality cannot be carried on if one segment of the feminist movement uses McCarthyite tactics to silence other voices," they wrote.[9] That was in 1982.

The point of rehearsing this history is to demonstrate that the phrase *politically correct* has always been double-edged. No sooner was it invoked as a genuine standard for sociopolitical practice—so that we might live as if the revolution had already happened—than it was mocked as purist, ideologically rigid, and authoritarian. Although the mainstream press is obviously trying to construct the phrase on a Stalinist "party line" model, there is little evidence of its use in the Old Left, and a great deal of evidence that within the New Left it was nearly always used with a double consciousness. Indeed, the fact that the phrase has survived with these self-mocking, ironized meanings is testimony to a kind of self-critical dimension to New Left politics, a flexibility, a suspiciousness of orthodoxy of any sort.

This history makes the current media campaign to discredit the Left especially infuriating. *Politically correct* has long been our own term of self-criticism. For George Bush and his hired hands—Cheney, Bennett, and D'Souza—to use the term places them squarely in the camp of the leather dykes, baiting the earnest. But the motive behind the current press campaign is hardly directed toward pleasure or knowledge. The timing of the campaign to discredit "political correctness" coincides with that other media event calculated to wipe out the sixties and to "kick the Vietnam syndrome": the Gulf War.

9. Ibid., 179–80.

The attack on the politically correct in the universities is an attack on the theory and practice of affirmative action – a legacy of the sixties and seventies – defined as the recruitment to an institution of students and faculty who do not conform to what has always constituted the population of academic institutions: usually white, middle class, straight, male. The cultural, or as some like to say, ideological, aspect of this practice has been the reassessment of whose culture is worth studying and knowing: whose history, whose literature, whose customs, whose attitudes, whose self-definitions. This investigation has created no little excitement in departments of history, literature, psychology, sociology – and even in a number of business schools. Certainly some part of the animus against the politically correct, as newly defined by the Right, has been generated by particular battles waged on those fronts. I would feel better about the campaign to expose the politically correct if the campaigners were willing to argue about the justice of affirmative action rather than the motives of those advocating this cultural adjustment.

For that's what the stakes are, just as they were in the late '60s at the beginning of the ferment: how to redistribute power, knowledge, and resources in this country. The appropriation of the New Left's in-joke by Bush and by the popular press, pretending to expose some narrow-minded doctrinaire position, is ludicrous in the face of the worsening economic and political position of women and African Americans in this country. Without rehearsing the depressing statistics about unemployment, salary scales, mortality, education levels, and the like, let me end by pointing out that insofar as the accusation of political correctness restrains or embarrasses anyone inclined to point out these appalling inequalities, the phrase is now successfully forestalling discussion of everything it ever stood for. In this Orwellian inversion, only those who uphold the conservative status quo are exempt from ridicule; only those who believe that the existing distribution of wealth and power is "natural," or inevitable, are depicted as operating without ideological bias. Like Goliath trying to disqualify

David by appealing to fair play, the government and the press are playing a disingenuous role in this contest. As our history reminds us, all we ever had were a few pebbles, and we've been polishing them for years. The point is to remember why we collected them in the first place.

NAS — Who Are These Guys, Anyway?

■ ■ ■

JACOB WEISBERG

■ ■ ■

As CONTROVERSIES over the canon, political correctness, and academic freedom continue to bedevil (and embarrass) the academy, NAS members are playing an increasingly visible role in the debate. The NAS itself has emerged as a significant force in American higher education. But where did it come from? Who joins? Who pays? And, finally, what is the NAS a force *for*?

Depending on whom you ask, you will get different answers about what the organization's mission is. Foremost among the things its members and directors say they want to do is preserve the established canon as a basis for the liberal arts curriculum. Beyond that, they want to defend traditional analytic methods and scholarly standards against "politicization" and "ideology." They are opposed to all "trendy methodologies" and have no truck with Marxism, feminism, new historicism, or deconstruction. They exist, at least in part, to fight the use of affirmative action in hiring and admissions decisions, and to defend academics unfairly accused of racism or sexism. The broad goal, in the words of NAS Chairman Herb London, who also ran last year as the Conservative candidate for governor in New York State, is nothing less than "to recapture the spirit of reasoned argument."

Though only four years old, the Princeton, New Jersey—based group has grown rapidly from a few hundred members to more than 1,700. With twenty-five state affiliates and plans for several

more, the NAS is on its way to becoming a full-scale counterin-
surgency by conservatives and traditionalists who consider themselves a disenfranchised minority within the academy. They have
emerged after years of relative quiescence and banded together in
the hopes of repelling those they see as "the barbarian in our
midst," in the memorable phrase of Alan C. Kors, a historian at
the University of Pennsylvania who is one of the group's stalwarts.

The NAS is engaged in a fight on many fronts. It runs a research center that keeps track of developments on campus and
maintains an executive- and faculty-search service to help place
like-minded teachers and administrators. The association also offers small two-year fellowships for "scholars engaged in serious
research" and publishes *Academic Questions,* a quarterly journal
with 3,000 subscribers, which Lynne Cheney, the conservative
chairman of the National Endowment for the Humanities, praises
as "one of the best written and best edited journals in the academic journal community." These endeavors are supported by a
$500,000-a-year budget, which comes mostly from grants from
conservative foundations, including the Coors Foundation in Colorado, the John M. Olin and Smith-Richardson foundations in
New York City, the Sarah Scaife Foundation in Pittsburgh, the
Institute for Educational Affairs in Washington, D.C., and the
Lynde and Harry Bradley Foundation in Milwaukee. "We're unlikely to get money from Ford or Rockefeller," notes Stephen
Balch, the NAS president, executive director, and one of its
founders.

The NAS grew out of a small New York City–area group called
the Campus Coalition for Democracy, which Balch, an associate
professor of government at the John Jay College of Criminal Justice, began in 1982. The coalition was intended as a support
group for people who felt they could not speak freely on issues of
concern to them, such as affirmative action and feminism, according to Barry Gross, a professor at CUNY's York College and
president of the New York Association of Scholars, the NAS's

largest affiliate. "We thought it was becoming increasingly difficult to hold any kind of rational arguments on certain kinds of topics," Gross says.

Among those who joined him early on were Peter Shaw, then a
professor emeritus in English at the State University of New York
at Stony Brook (he currently teaches at St. Peter's College), Herb
London, dean of the Gallatin Division of New York University,
and Carol Iannone, a professor of English in the Gallatin Division. "We did not constitute a minyan," remembers London. "I
said I didn't think we'd find ten like-minded people in the entire
country's university system. I was quite wrong. There was a responsive audience out there of people who felt that the university
had abdicated primary responsibility to pass the canon on from
one generation to another."

Galvanized by attacks on the core curriculum at Stanford and
elsewhere, Balch and his colleagues decided to found a national
organization in 1987. "When he spoke to me and a few others
about founding an organization, we didn't have to spend too much
time talking about it," Shaw recalls. "Scholarship and teaching
had come to be dominated by leftist political ideology. I didn't
think there was much prospect of success. There was an atmosphere of intolerance and intimidation when it came to ideas such
as ours, in favor of a more traditional, humanistically inclined
kind of teaching that wasn't based on politics. People were afraid
to declare themselves in opposition to new trends lest they be labeled reactionary, sexist, or racist."

Balch says that he and his colleagues shared a feeling that academic culture was becoming increasingly one-sided, politicized,
dominated by an adversarial mentality that held "all the major institutions of American society to be deeply flawed and chronically
unjust." They objected to the use of the classroom to "inculcate a
narrow and sectarian type of politics, rather than using it to ac-
quaint students with a wide range of views," according to Balch.
Stanley Rothman, a political scientist at Smith who has become
active in the group, agrees. "There's a lot of junk going on," he

says, "that is weakening the scholarly tradition of the university and has begun to impair [its] effectiveness."

The best record of what has concerned the NAS over four years of existence is its journal, *Academic Questions*, edited by London. The first issue, published in the winter of 1987, began with London's "call to the academy," an argument that "radicals, despite their influence, are less dangerous to the campus atmosphere than the liberal majority that has manifestly surrendered to the pressures of vocal opinion."

The journal consistently returns to a few themes. Academic feminism, in its various manifestations, is attacked in almost every issue. An article by Boston University sociologist Brigitte Berger equates the work of feminist Evelyn Fox Keller with Nazi physics. Peace studies, the Critical Legal Studies movement, African and Latin American studies, deconstruction, new historicism, ethical investment policies, and Paul Starr's *The Social Transformation of American Medicine* are all subject to broadsides by regular contributors to *Commentary* and the *National Review*. Articles defend Allan Bloom from his critics and castigate law school faculty for opposing Robert Bork's nomination to the Supreme Court. There is praise for Jeane Kirkpatrick and William Bennett, whom London calls "the Winston Churchill of American Education." One attack on affirmative action philosophy is by Michael Levin, a philosophy professor at the City College of New York, who has since achieved notoriety by suggesting that black students in New York ride in separate, police-occupied subway cars. (Levin was asked to resign from the organization's board of directors after the controversy surfaced.)

While a number of the pieces in the journal are well argued, too many others are sneering and ill-tempered, or even slightly nutty. One article by Lawrence A. Beyer of Tulane Law School goes on at length about the pernicious effects of highlighters ("those marking pens that allow readers to emphasize passages in their books with transparent overlays of bright color"). More often, the intellectual style of *Academic Questions* echoes the high dudgeon of *Contentions*, the polemical newsletter of the recently dissolved neoconservative Committee for the Free World. In the Spring 1990 issue, London rants about Ford Foundation support for feminist fringe groups "which, endowed by angels at the Ford Foundation, . . . become the angels and benefactors of their peers. Is it any wonder that the curriculum is in disarray and the defenders of Western civilization are often hiding in their office bunkers?" The aggrieved tone makes it unlikely that the magazine will persuade anyone who is not already in the NAS camp.

The NAS put on its largest conference ever at the New York Penta Hotel last June. The three-day event, whose theme was "Strategies for the Nineties," was attended by 300 people and covered by the *Chronicle of Higher Education*, the *American Spectator*, and others. According to reports, the conference oscillated between political sermonizing and more-measured analysis. It began with a blast of the former during a panel called "Academic Utopianism: Its Past and Its Future," headlined by Midge Decter, former director of the Committee for the Free World, Paul Craig Roberts of the Center for Strategic and International Studies, and Gertrude Himmelfarb, a professor emeritus at the CUNY Graduate School.

Much of the conference revolved around tales of academic persecution. The NAS presented its $2,500 Sidney Hook Award for "uncommon service in the defense of intellectual freedom and academic integrity" to James Coleman, a University of Chicago sociologist, who described difficulties he encountered as a result of his research into racial integration, which found black schoolteachers to be less well prepared than their white counterparts. Stephan Thernstrom, the Winthrop Professor of History at Harvard, described how he was tarred by the accusation of racism after students accused him of "racial insensitivity." The charge stemmed from his use of the politically incorrect terms *American Indians* and *Oriental*. Thernstrom attributed the failure of liberal colleagues to come to his defense to a pervasive fear of the taint of racism through association. Donald Kagan, the dean of Yale College, spoke of opposition to his nomination based on his conservative politics. Joseph Horn, a former associate dean at the College of Liberal Arts at the University of Texas, told of being asked to resign because of his candid opposition to affirmative action and multiculturalism.

The overall emphasis of the conference was on organizing and "fighting back." Kagan recommended that scientists be enlisted in the struggle to defend the liberal arts. "Scientists believe in the efficacy of reason and the possibility of truth. Get *them* involved in the total life of the institution. Reach out to your scientific colleagues: they will be especially good in holding to high standards." The point was enthusiastically seconded by Robert Gordon of Johns Hopkins, who urged in the question period that scientists not be left to muse on the sidelines. "Radicalize them!" When demands for multiculturalism and feminism come full steam at you, Gordon counseled: "Yell, Physics and mathematics first!"

The conference concluded with a panel that addressed the question "Can the Professoriate Reform Itself?" The discussion included calls to arms by Gross and Kors. "From administrators who are quiescent careerists or just plain scared, to tenured radicals, through self-appointed student leaders and uncomprehending newspapers, battle is given on every front," Gross told the audience.

Kors exhorted his "pessimistic" colleagues "to become the monasteries of a new dark ages, preserving what is worth preserving amid the barbaric ravages in the countryside and the towns of academe."

The feeling that they are the only ones who can keep the flame of learning alive while marauding radicals rape and pillage the academy is, in fact, what appears to unite a membership that ranges from social conservatives to neoconservatives, libertarians, and even a few liberals. According to John Agresto, president of St. John's College, who spoke at the conference, "What holds the organization together is a feeling of being beleaguered by forces who feel nothing but contempt for Western civilization both as a course and as a political fact."

But is the NAS's overall portrayal of the university – one endlessly repeated and amplified by the general press – accurate?

"To read the things being written by some of those people, you'd think Shakespeare was holed up in a cave in Montana because everyone wants to kill him, that Milton had been driven out of the academy by Zane Grey," says the celebrated "barbarian" Stanley Fish.

"I think theirs is a highly distorted picture that overlooks both social and intellectual developments on the campus," notes Catharine Stimpson, dean of the graduate school at Rutgers. Stimpson argues that the NAS betrays a naive view that the academic canon is formed by all but the most excellent texts being weeded out. In her view, the canon is created through a complex interaction of historical and social as well as intellectual forces. "I don't think the university is going to decline like a corrupt Atlantis because we open up the canon," Stimpson says. "To expand the canon is to enhance culture, not destroy it."

Waxing hysterical about the end of Western civilization, the NAS does tend to disregard the size of its own base of support. Members seldom talk about the places where the traditional liberal arts has suffered few inroads. And they refuse to take solace in the enormous success of books like Allan Bloom's *The Closing of the American Mind* and E. D. Hirsch's *Cultural Literacy*.

In fact, what documentation exists suggests that academics are not nearly as radical as NAS members believe. According to a 1984 study by the Carnegie Foundation for the Advancement of Teaching, a mere 5.8 percent of 5,000 teachers surveyed considered themselves "left," as opposed to 33.8 percent who considered themselves "liberal," 26.6 who said they were "middle of the road," 29.6 percent who said they were "moderately conservative," and 4.2 percent who claimed to be "strongly conservative." This represents a slight shift to the right since 1969. Daniel Bell, professor emeritus in sociology at Harvard, argues that left-wing influence has been diminishing in the social sciences, and to a lesser extent in the humanities as well.

On the question of the curriculum's evolution, the NAS may have a better case. However, while examples of fatuous course offerings are legion, no one has proven that fewer students are reading Plato or Shakespeare than in the past. In an attempt to bolster its contention, the NAS is now studying the undergraduate curriculum at fifty top-flight public and private colleges for a report on how it has changed over twenty-five years. The results are not yet in.

The NAS claims to defend free inquiry and unqualified debate in the tradition of J. S. Mill, Justice Holmes, Robert Maynard Huchins, and Lionel Trilling. The group exists in part, London says, to "promote the idea of rational exegesis." But members are likely to denounce alien ideas more often than they engage or consider them. As Gross told the Penta gathering, "The litany of maledictions and nonsense is familiar to us all: pluralism, diversity, role model, the canon, male hegemony, elitism, awareness, value neutrality, insensitivity, banned speech, deconstructed texts."

The NAS is also prone to conflating its admirable intellectual ideals with far less compelling political prejudices. In conversation, members of the association blur the distinction between vigorous debate about the ideas that undergird Western democracy and agreement with those ideas. They want students to ask basic questions but object when the answers derived are not the "right" ones.

The NAS has already had an impact on American higher education and is likely to become a more significant force in the future. But its potential for growth may be limited by its political slant. So far, the group has failed to attract many moderates or liberals, who ought to be broadly sympathetic to the group's goals.

The Jacques Barzuns and Mortimer Adlers, the Irving Howes and Daniel Bells, have kept their distance. Bell, for example, says he approves of the basic ideas behind the NAS but is put off by the group's stridency. "A group that was more moderate, cool, willing to make relevant distinctions, would get a great deal of support," he says. "Unfortunately, aggressiveness, tackiness seem to win out."

All that was in evidence at the Penta conference, sometimes memorably. During the response period at one of the Penta sessions, a young white male assistant professor rose to complain about admissions offices that admit students on the basis of social-policy considerations rather than scholarly aptitude. As he spoke, the ubiquitous conference photographer approached from one side, knelt down, and snapped a picture. The moment the flashbulb went off, the professor reflexively raised his hand to cover his face, and a nervous laugh rippled through the room. The professor spun around and faced the audience directly. "Look," he said, pointing at his chest. "*I'm* not a member of a protected group."

The Funding of the NAS

■ ■ ■

SARA DIAMOND

■ ■ ■

T HE NATIONAL ASSOCIATION of Scholars is the first
concerted effort to organize right-wing faculty. NAS began in
1987, but its genealogy can be traced to the Institute for Educational Affairs, founded in 1978 by neoconservative writer Irving
Kristol and former Treasury Secretary William Simon. IEA has
since served as a conduit for corporate funding of selected aca
demics. (In September 1990, IEA changed its name to the Madison Center for Educational Affairs.)

IEA–Madison Center is bankrolled by corporate foundations,
including Coors, Mobil, Smith-Richardson, Earhart, Scaife, and
Olin. IEA board members — some of whom are also trustees of
contributing foundations — dole out respectable sums to up-and-
coming graduate students and junior faculty, according to the
minutes of one IEA meeting, "to give their work impact and promote their careers."

From the start, IEA differed from an "Old Right" academic
project, the Intercollegiate Studies Institute, started in 1952 by
associates of William F. Buckley, Jr. ISI continues to hold con-
ferences and publish a slew of journals, but the articles are too
philosophical and lackluster to attract much attention.

IEA is the force behind a crop of sixty provocative tabloids
published on fifty-seven campuses. The most notorious, the *Dartmouth Review,* has repeatedly drawn fire for its bigoted invec-
tives. In 1986, on Martin Luther King, Jr.'s birthday, *Review*
staffers tore down shanties built by the college's anti-apartheid

groups. In a stunt timed for the 1990 Yom Kippur holiday, the *Review* published a quotation from Hitler's *Mein Kampf* on its masthead. Dartmouth president James Freedman responded by denouncing the paper—and its outside agitators William F. Buckley, Jr., Pat Buchanan, George Gilder, and William Rusher—in a *New York Times* op-ed. But while the spotlight has been fixed in IEA's irritating student press, its intellectual authors have quietly laid the groundwork for more insidious means of putting liberal and progressive academics on the defensive.

According to a set of documents I've obtained, the immediate predecessor to the NAS was a group called the Campus Coalition for Democracy, headquartered, like NAS, in Princeton. The Coalition began in 1982 and was headed by Stephen H. Balch, a professor of government at the City University of New York. (Balch later became president of NAS.) In 1983 the Campus Coalition held a conference at Long Island University, attended by about 120 people. The subject was Central America and the list of speakers was impressive. Jeane Kirkpatrick gave the plenary address. Panel speakers included Assistant Secretary of State Elliott Abrams, Penn Kemble of the Institute on Religion and Democracy, Michael Ledeen of the Center for Strategic and International Studies, William Doherty of the American Institute for Free Labor Development (AIFLD), and contra leader Arturo Cruz. The conference program acknowledged funding from the Long Island University John P. McGrath Fund and from the Committee for the Free World.

The Committee for the Free World, headed by Elliott Abrams's mother-in-law, Midge Decter, was at the time one of the most important assets in the Reagan administration's war against Nicaragua. It turns out the CFW was also involved in securing funding for the nascent faculty organizing projects. Campus Coalition president Stephen Balch solicited advice from CFW's Steven Munson on getting money from IEA.

By late 1984 the campus organizing plan was spelled out in a

confidential memo, "The Report on the Universities," written by
Roderic R. Richardson for the Smith-Richardson Foundation.
(It's worth noting that this foundation has had a history of sponsoring CIA-linked media projects and leadership training programs for CIA and Defense Department personnel.) The document proposed to distinguish between two possible anti-Left
strategies: "deterrence activism" and "high-ground articulation," also termed "idea marketing." Deterrence activism, wrote
Richardson, "exists purely in response to the left-wing agenda. It
is not very interesting, frankly, boring, and it is the kind of activism sponsored heretofore. At best it is a form of cheerleading that
can focus some attention on stirring media events."

Instead, Richardson advocated "high-ground activism" or "articulation, the attempt to steal one or another highground away
from the left, by both action and articulation. As noted, it involves doing things like insisting on rigorous discussion and de
bates, setting up political unions, battling divestiture and other
causes, not by calling their goals wrong, necessarily, but by pro-
posing better ways of solving the problem. Student journalism is a
high-ground approach."

Richardson recommended that the Right "mimic left-wing organization" by forming what he called Regional Resource Centers, starting with a faculty network in one area of the country,
say, New England or around New York. "The aim of such a group
is to set up a permanent network, to defuse the Left, to grab the
high ground, to change the atmosphere on campuses, and perhaps to help command a corner of the national agenda."

Richardson wrote that he already had support for his plan, but
he warned that "the New Right, perceiving a vacuum, might well
try to take over the student activist and journalism movements."

Before the Regional Resources Center plan could get off the
ground, a faction further to the right than Richardson and IEA
launched Accuracy in Academia. A spin-off of Reed Irvine's
Accuracy in Media, AIA recruited classroom spies and began

compiling a data base on professors AIA labeled "left-wing propagandists." AIA's first executive director, Les Csorba, was a 22-year-old activist fresh from the University of California at Davis, where he had organized a harassment campaign against visiting lecturer Saul Landau in 1985. AIA president John LeBoutillier, a former member of Congress, was then a leader of the World Anti-Communist League (WACL), as were three other members of AIA's initial advisory board. Irvine had at one time been prominent within WACL. At the time of AIA's founding in 1985, WACL was one of the most important coordinating bodies for death squad activities in Central America and elsewhere.

Not because of these connections, but because of its pitbull tactics, AIA attracted plenty of media attention and earned itself a reputation as campus "thought police."

Among AIA's strongest detractors were fellow rightists, including Midge Decter of the Committee for the Free World. In a December 1985 *New York Times* op-ed, Decter expressed agreement with Irvine's view of the professorate, but charged AIA with mimicking 1960s radicals who had turned the universities into "a veritable hotbed of reckless, mindless anti-Americanism." Advocating the "high-ground" strategy of her colleagues at the Smith-Richardson Foundation, Decter wrote, "The only way to deal with words and ideas and teachings one deplores is to offer better words and ideas and teachings."

Decter projected herself as a true believer in "academic freedom" when, in fact, she and her ilk were motivated less by civil libertarianism than by the shrewd understanding that the most effective ideological warfare strategy is that which sneaks up on its enemy slowly. AIA was such a crude and noisy operation that it might have discredited – and thereby slowed – other right-wing strategies.

But not for long. In 1986, Decter's *Commentary* magazine published an important article: "The Tenured Left" by Stephen H. Balch and Herbert I. London (who in 1987 would become the founders of the National Association of Scholars). Balch was then associate professor of government at the John Jay College of Criminal Justice in New York. Herbert London was, and is, dean of the Gallatin Division of New York University, as well as a fellow of the Pentagon-funded Hudson Institute in Indiana. Balch and London expressed their distaste for Accuracy in Academia by making a phony analogy between it and the campus anti-apartheid movement. The only difference, as far as Balch and London could see, was that AIA's efforts, "unlike those of the divestiture campaign, have been wholly confined to the realm of public criticism, neither fomenting disruption, nor toying with the possibilities of violent confrontation, nor obliging university administrators or faculty members to adopt an institutional stand."

Their argument continued: anti-apartheid protesters were getting slaps on the wrists, while AIA activists were labeled troublemakers. And all because the academy is dominated by leftists. Among the "evidence" presented, Balch and London reported an incident in 1985 when the *American Sociological Review* had given its lead article space to a real live Marxist – who also happened to be an associate editor of the journal. The Marxist in question was UC Berkeley sociologist Michael Burawoy. Balch and London trashed Burawoy's field study of a Hungarian manufacturing plant because the work was done in collaboration with Janos Lukacs, of the Hungarian Academy of Sciences. The logic was that Burawoy's work could not be scientifically valid so long as his fellow sociologist was a citizen in a communist regime. (Presumably, Balch and London would now approve work by Burawoy and Lukacs, since Hungary has turned toward capitalism.)

Still, the tactic was to red-bait particular scholars. By 1987 the Right's anti-progressive argument was broadened with the publication of Allan Bloom's best-seller, *The Closing of the American Mind*. With generous funding from the Earhart and Olin foundations, Bloom's book constructed a case against the concept of "cultural relativism," propagated by leftist intellectuals, but manifested throughout society in everything from too little Bible reading to too much rock 'n' roll. Bloom attributed the dumbing-down of the U.S. citizenry to a gradual erosion of ethnocentric prejudices. "Cultural relativism," he wrote, "succeeds in destroying the West's universal or intellectually imperialistic claims, leaving it to be just another culture."

In late 1987 the National Association of Scholars (NAS) was formally inaugurated, with Herbert London named chair of the board and Stephen Balch, president. Among the prominent board members are Leslie Lenkowsky, formerly research director of the Smith-Richardson Foundation, who was at one time acting director of the U.S. Information Agency. Lenkowsky directed IEA until 1990, when he left to become president of the Hudson Institute, the current hangout for former drug czar William Bennett.

A preliminary survey of tax returns from some of the same right-wing foundations that bankroll IEA shows NAS with an annual budget well in excess of a quarter of a million dollars.

The first few issues of the NAS's quarterly journal, *Academic Questions*, took aim at feminist scholarship, affirmative action, supposed leftist control of Latin American, African, and Asian studies programs, and even student evaluations of professors. Recent articles are even more broadbrushed in approach. One six-page article lamented college students' use of highlighter pens. Beyond its surface absurdity, the real point of the article was that students should not be so free to pick and choose what *they think* they need to remember from any assigned reading. The argument underlying a fall 1990 article on "the radical politicization of liberal education" relies on a patently false assertion. John Agresto, president of St. John's College in New Mexico, claims that radicals deny the possibility of reading texts "nonpolitically" because they deny "transtemporal and universal truths or principles."

NAS has taken credit for the repeal of a University of Michigan speech code—intended to reduce racist and sexist incidents on campus. With support from the NAS and the Michigan chapter of the ACLU, Wesley Wynne, a graduate student in biological psychology, sued his alma mater and won. In 1989, a federal court ruled that UM's speech code was so broadly defined as to threaten the First Amendment.

According to a favorable article in the *Chronicle of Higher Education*, NAS now has 1,400 members, statewide affiliates in seventeen states, and campus chapters at the Universities of Minnesota at Twin Cities, New Mexico at Albuquerque, Texas at Austin, and at Duke and Emory Universities. And NAS has some concrete plans to expand its influence.

In early 1990 all NAS members received a thirty-eight-page questionnaire prepared by the affiliated Madison Center, founded in 1988 by Allan Bloom and then Secretary of Education William Bennett. (In September 1990 the Center merged with the Institute for Educational Affairs and is now known as the hybrid Madison Center for Educational Affairs.) The survey is an amazingly thorough intelligence-gathering tool. Respondents are asked to provide detailed answers to questions such as: How often does the administration play an active role in tenure decisions? What are the prevailing attitudes toward ROTC and CIA recruitment on campus? How conspicuous is the homosexual faculty presence on campus?

Some of the data found its way into *The Commonsense Guide to American Colleges: 1991–1992*. The guide focuses on "how education and teaching has fared under the mixed influences of the last fifteen or twenty years," says Madison Center president Charles Horner, a former State Department, U.S. Information Agency, and RAND Corporation official.

NAS has set up a Research Center in Princeton—consistent with the 1984 Richardson plan—to "accumulate information on the issues and trends of contemporary higher education." In its fall 1990 newsletter, the NAS appealed to its members to send in course descriptions and proposals, departmental newsletters, and the like, for trend analysis to be conducted by NAS research director Glenn Ricketts.

The survey data from the Madison Center will come in handy as the NAS implements a couple of its other plans. One is the new Faculty and Executive Search Service, which is a mini-employment service provided free to NAS members. Another strategy is the formation of caucuses within the professional associations organized by various academic disciplines. Already, the NAS and the Intercollegiate Studies Institute have formed anti-liberal groupings within the Modern Language Association, the American Historical Association, and the American Philosophical Association, according to ISI national director Chris Long.

A November 1990 mailing to the Sociology-Anthropology section of the NAS, from Dan McMurry of Middle Tennessee State University, spelled out an effort to "reform from within" the American Sociological Association (ASA). Hardly a hotbed of radicalism, the ASA exists to promote the careers of its members, who are mostly mild-mannered theorists more interested in studying the world than changing it. The NAS plans to begin sponsoring special sessions at ASA meetings. How convenient — the current president of the ASA is University of Chicago Professor James S. Coleman, a prominent member of NAS. The "Dear Colleague" letter warned NAS members to "avoid being regarded as conservative. We hope to cast our nets widely."

What Happened at Harvard

■ ■ ■

JON WIENER

■ ■ ■

THE NEOCON BOOK of the year is Dinesh D'Souza's *Illiberal Education*, which spent much of the spring and the entire summer of 1991 on the best-seller list, promising readers an encyclopedia of offenses perpetrated on campus in the name of "political correctness." Reviewers of the book have highlighted the case of Harvard historian Stephan Thernstrom as one of D'Souza's most illuminating. Eugene Genovese wrote in the *New Republic* that Thernstrom had been "savaged for political incorrectness in the classroom." *New York* magazine featured Thernstrom as a victim of "demagogic and fanatical" black students. C. Vann Woodward, writing in the *New York Review of Books*, cited the Thernstrom case as an example of "the attack on freedom . . . led by minorities."

As D'Souza tells the story, Thernstrom, widely known on campus as a liberal, was charged by three black students with "racial insensitivity" in his lectures in an introductory history course, The Peopling of America. Instead of coming to him with their complaints, they went to an administrative committee and to the student newspaper, the *Harvard Crimson*. The greatest offense came not from the black students but from the Harvard administration: Dean of the College Fred Jewett, according to D'Souza, issued a statement that suggested that the college backed the students against Thernstrom. Dean of the Faculty Michael Spence eventually stated that, in D'Souza's words, "no disciplinary action would be taken against Thernstrom," but Spence did "praise the course of action of Thernstrom's accusers as 'judicious and fair.'" Thernstrom was so discouraged by the student attack and the administration's failure to defend his academic freedom that he decided not to teach the course again. Thus the Thernstrom case provided D'Souza, Woodward, Genovese, and others with what they said was an example of a distinguished liberal professor hounded out of teaching his course by an alliance of militant black students and the administrators who supported them.

In fact, almost every element of the story D'Souza tells is erroneous. "I talked with one of the students who had complained about Thernstrom," says Orlando Patterson, professor of sociology at Harvard. "She was genuinely upset about one of his lectures. This was not an ideological reaction, it was a personal and emotional one. She said she did not want to make it a political issue, and had deliberately rejected attempts by more political students to make it into a cause. She was trembling with rage at the *Crimson* for making this public. She said that when Thernstrom was lecturing on the black family, she understood him to be asking why black men treat their women so badly. I assumed that he had offered a straightforward statement of sociological fact. I told her it's increasingly problematic to have an objective discussion of the black family. We talked for a long time, and in the end she came around to seeing what I was trying to say. I told her I was sure Steve wasn't a racist, and suggested she go talk to him about how she felt. She did. They had a long talk, shook hands and that was the end of it. But the *Crimson* had made it into a political issue."

Paula Ford is one of the students who complained about Thernstrom; today she is enrolled at Harvard Law School. D'Souza never interviewed her, she says. Although he reported that the students never complained directly to Thernstrom, she says she and several of her friends talked to Thernstrom after class "a couple of times"—especially after his lecture on the black family. She recalls that "he said black men beat their wives, and then their wives kicked them out. We complained to him after class that this was offensive and inaccurate. He said, 'If you don't believe me, read Toni Morrison.' I felt that was completely trivializing what's out there." She and one other student then went to the campus race relations committee and said, "We have this problem, how do we deal with this?" Today she recalls, "It was a difficult and emotional process for us. A good part of the campus felt, 'They're professors. Why are you accusing them?'"

Regarding Thernstrom's decision not to teach the course again, Ford said she was "surprised" and "not happy" to hear it. "That was not our goal. Our goal was to point out areas in his lectures that we thought were inaccurate and possibly could be changed. To me, it's a big overreaction for him to decide not to teach the course again because of that."

Wendi Grantham is quoted by D'Souza as one of the students who complained about Thernstrom. She graduated in 1989; today she is studying drama in New York City. D'Souza never interviewed her, she says. "If he had, I would have made it clear to him that I was not one of the students who filed the complaint. I didn't even know they were filing a complaint. A reporter for the *Crimson* led me to believe this complaint was public, which turned out not to be true. All I said was that I could see that their complaint might have some basis."

Eventually she wrote a letter to the *Crimson* explaining her position. "People don't understand the term *racial insensitivity*," she told me. "It's not a charge of bigotry or racism. I said in my letter to the *Crimson*, 'I do not charge that Thernstrom is a racist.' We did question some things in his course because his perspective on black life came across to us as simplistic and not reflective of our own experience. You can't always anticipate other people's experience, but you can learn from listening to them. In most academic situations the professor puts out the knowledge and that's it. But I think some things ought to be questioned."

D'Souza writes that black students criticized the course for using slave owners' journals; Thernstrom told him, "It is essential for young people to hear what justifications the slave owners supplied for their actions." "I agree completely with that," Grantham said. "The problem I had was with the absence of the slave perspective to put alongside the planter perspective. Why not read the slave narratives to get the other side of the story? There's a lot of them available, but Professor Thernstrom didn't assign any. This was a general studies course; for most white students, this was all the black history they would ever get. We felt the knowledge this course would give them was inadequate.

"I finally did go speak to Professor Thernstrom," she said. "I said I was sorry if he was scapegoated; I did not want to penalize him but I did want to raise questions about his perspective. It was never my intention to stop Thernstrom from teaching this course. If that's what he chooses to do, it's his decision."

D'Souza didn't interview any of the students in the Thernstrom case, but he did approach three other black students majoring in Afro-American studies. I located one of them: Tiya Miles, returning to Harvard as a senior this fall [1991]. "When he talked to us, we had the impression he was putting together some kind of statistical report. We had no idea what his political slant was. We were happy that somebody was going to talk about the problems of race on campuses like Harvard. He didn't tell us anything about what he did at Dartmouth or on the *Dartmouth Review*. I wish I had known that this was a situation in which I had to protect myself."

D'Souza quotes Miles and her two friends as examples of the "impact of the race and gender pedagogy." The three Afro-Am majors come off as lamentably ignorant, in contrast to the wise and well-informed interviewer. They know nothing about Lincoln's view of the Declaration of Independence, a subject on which D'Souza showed he was an expert. "But we were all new on the campus," Miles points out. When D'Souza talked to them, the three women were all first-year students who had completed one semester of college. Their ignorance couldn't have been an effect of the "impact" of Afro-American studies, as D'Souza claims, because they had barely begun to study the subject. Miles concluded, "I don't understand how a person of color can take his position."

The strongest criticism from D'Souza, Woodward, and Genovese is aimed not at the black students who complained about
Thernstrom but rather at the Harvard administration for its conduct in the case. Because he received so little support from the
administration, Thernstrom told D'Souza, "I felt like a rape victim." D'Souza writes that "a few days after the Thernstrom incident, Dean of the College Fred Jewett issued an open letter to the
Harvard community. . . . Far from coming to his defense, Jewett
appeared to give full administrative sanction to the charges
against Thernstrom."

Jewett today remains Dean of the College at Harvard. D'Souza
never interviewed him, Jewett says: "My statement had nothing to
do with Thernstrom. As I recall, it was distributed in registration
envelopes at beginning of term, a couple of weeks before anything
about Thernstrom became news. It was titled 'Open Letter on Racial Harassment.' There had been some incidents on campus of
swastika paintings, and a few incidents involving the police that
had created some concerns. So we felt we needed a strong general
statement on harassment. Obviously the Thernstrom case was not
in that category. When students disagree with the ideas presented
by a professor, they are not dealing with harassment, they are
dealing with academic freedom. That's not something that the
university should interfere with."

The other administrator criticized in the book and the reviews,
Spence, is today graduate dean of the business school at Stanford.
Woodward repeats D'Souza's claim that Spence "praised
[Thernstrom's] accusers as 'judicious and fair.'" Woodward left
out the crucial part of the dean's statement, as did D'Souza: the
dean said that the students who complained "have avoided public
comment. . . . That course of action seems to me judicious and
fair." It was not the criticism of Thernstrom that was "judicious
and fair" but rather the students' decision not to go public with
their criticism that the dean praised.

According to D'Souza, in the same statement the dean declared that "no disciplinary action would be taken" against
Thernstrom. In fact, the issue of disciplinary action against

Thernstrom was not mentioned in the dean's statement; on the contrary, the dean declared that "[in] disputes over classroom material . . . instructors exercise full discretion over the content of lectures and the conduct of classroom discussion," and "in the classroom, our students are entitled to question views with which they disagree," and finally, "the University cannot prevent all of the conflicts that a commitment to free inquiry may provoke." Thernstrom found this statement to be "equivocal at best," D'Souza reports, interpreting it to mean that "he had the right to be racist, if he wished." Genovese agreed, writing that the Harvard administrators in the Thernstrom case were "doing their best to create an atmosphere in which professors who value their reputations . . . learn to censor themselves."

As for the three students who took their complaint to the university's Advisory Committee on Race Relations, they were advised that the committee had no jurisdiction over professors' teaching, and that they should take their complaint to Thernstrom—which they did. "They felt the university didn't do anything to back up their concerns," Dean Jewett said.

If D'Souza's account of the Thernstrom case is misleading, it's a model of restraint compared with other accounts of the same events. *New York* magazine began its article on the case with what appeared to be a description of black students verbally harassing Thernstrom as he walked around the campus:

"'Racist.' 'Racist!' 'The man is a racist!' A *racist!*' Such denunciations, hissed in tones of self-righteousness and contempt, vicious and vengeful, furious, smoking with hatred—such denunciations haunted Stephan Thernstrom for weeks."

When I asked Thernstrom if this passage was accurate, he replied, "I was appalled when I first saw that. Nothing like that ever happened." He described that passage as "artistic license, describing how it felt to be Thernstrom in that period, and that part is absolutely true." (The piece does go on to say, "He found it hard not to image the pointing fingers.") The *Crimson*, he said, "ran a story just about every day, with headlines like 'Thernstrom's racial insensitivity still in doubt.'" It's not hard to understand why he would be upset and angry about this press coverage, but, as he acknowledged, "There are freedom of press issues where the *Crimson* is involved."

According to Thernstrom and his defenders, the final result of black student complaints is that, in the words of *New York* magazine, his course "is no longer offered at Harvard." But that is only because Thernstrom himself decided not to offer it. No black student or organization ever demanded, much less suggested, that Thernstrom not teach the course. Nevertheless, Thernstrom describes himself as a victim of McCarthyism. In Thernstrom's case, three students complained that he had been "racially insensitive" in his lectures, and he responded by refusing to teach the course again. Under McCarthyism, professors didn't voluntarily decide not to teach after being criticized by students; they were prevented from teaching—fired—after being criticized by the government.

In an interview Thernstrom agreed with several of these points. The students who complained about him "wanted to keep it a secret," he said. The administration gave them no satisfaction: "They were told, 'We don't take complaints against the faculty; have you talked to him? If not, do so.' That was the end." The students eventually did come to see him; one meeting was "very formal and cold," while the other was "quite a nice conversation." He agreed that no one had asked, much less demanded, that he not teach the course. He said it was correct that he did not assign slave narratives, because "my focus is more demographic and economic."

As for the administration's public statements, he said that Dean Spence was "very sympathetic; his end-of-the-year report was very strong"—even though D'Souza reports that Thernstrom regarded Spence's statement as "equivocal at best." As for Dean Jewett's statement on racial harassment, "Later I heard that his document had been in the works for a long time and was not issued as some kind of comment on this matter at all." Thernstrom said he still wasn't certain, and had never asked Jewett—even though he told D'Souza (as D'Souza then reported) that Jewett had "issued the 'open letter' against Thernstrom."

I asked Thernstrom whether he thought black students had criticized him because of his stand on affirmative action. "I am critical of affirmative action," he said, "but I don't think that was clear to them. I didn't lecture on affirmative action. They didn't know what I thought. The complaint was purely internal to the course."

Thernstrom said he remains incensed that Assistant Dean of the College for Race Relations and Minority Affairs Hilda Hernandez-Gravelle "helped these students" prepare their complaint. "I've made clear my dislike for her and her role, and have taken to monitoring her program, AWARE Week," he said. "I made an appearance at a couple of AWARE sessions to make it clear that I'm keeping an eye on them."

Hernandez-Gravelle commented, "I think it's really sad that a person would use his energy in such a persecutory and uncollegial manner. This office is about creating dialogue, helping everyone understand different perspectives and ways of recognizing and appreciating the issues. It's appropriate for me to advise and assist students by presenting them with the alternatives they have in addressing their issues. Without commenting specifically on this case, I can say I may help a student write a letter if that is appropriate; I may suggest that it is not necessarily appropriate to accuse a person of being a racist; it might be better to inform him of your reaction to something he said."

What more could Thernstrom have wanted the Harvard administration to do, beyond issuing statements affirming his academic freedom? President Derek Bok, he replied, might have "declared that Harvard selects its faculty with enormous care and backs with great confidence the freedom of its professors to discuss subjects in which they are competent"; the administration "might have come out swinging" at the students who criticized him, Thernstrom said.

D'Souza represents the finest flower of a vast neocon talent search, one that began early in the Reagan era, when right-wing foundations like Olin set up and funded a network of conservative student newspapers, the flagship of which was the virulently racist *Dartmouth Review*, where D'Souza first demonstrated his talents as editor in chief. After graduation, the most promising of these young men were given positions in the Reagan White House (where D'Souza held the title Domestic Policy Analyst) and later in conservative think tanks like the American Enterprise Institute (where D'Souza wrote his book under a grant from the Olin Foundation). After ten years of searching for and cultivating young neocon ideologues, the Olin Foundation and the American Enterprise Institute finally got everything they could have hoped for in Dinesh D'Souza and his book: a best-seller attacking multiculturalism and the campus left and, best of all, a right-wing book written by a young person of color.

But if D'Souza's account of the Thernstrom case is typical of his work, *Illiberal Education* rests on a morass of inaccuracies, exaggerations, and falsehoods. John Womack, who had chaired the Harvard history department before the complaint against Thernstrom surfaced, comments, "There had been a case years ago at Harvard involving Richard Herrnstein, who had his classroom disrupted and was harassed in the Yard [by students who objected to his writing about race and I.Q.]. But nobody did anything to Steve except say he had been insensitive. You'd think, 'Jesus, he ought to be able to get over that.' Instead, Steve just weirded out. He became very combative. He acted as if his very reputation as a liberal was being wiped out. It's easy to see why the *New Republic* picked it up, but why Gene Genovese or Vann Woodward would get on the bandwagon is more puzzling. To my amazement, this has now become an issue that stands in the annals of free speech."

"There is no Thernstrom case," concludes Martin Kilson, professor of government at Harvard. "There were 680 black students at Harvard at the time. A couple of them complained about his interpretations of black experience. That got translated into an attack on freedom of speech by black students. Nothing like that ever happened at Harvard. It's a marvelous example of the skill of the neocons at taking small events and translating them into weapons against the pluralistic thrust on American campuses."

What Happened at SUNY

■ ■ ■

DAVID BEERS

■ ■ ■

THE GROWING CONSENSUS that vocal disagreement
with the Right's agenda had devolved into brownshirt tactics
was no accident, but rather the result of a very small political
campaign to make conservative ideologues on campus appear to
be victims of oppression. In telling who helped orchestrate it, and
how, the State University of New York at Binghamton is a good
place to start.

This much all sides agree upon: in Spring 1991, members of
Binghamton's new NAS chapter advertised a kickoff lecture on
the fall of the Berlin Wall. Professors Richard Hofferbert and
Saul Levin would speak. A false rumor had it that the Ku Klux
Klan might attend, gossip of unknown origin but fueled by the fact
that Hofferbert had invited a Klan member to address his class
two years before. Some two hundred students, along with leftist
lecturer Gonzalo Santos, arrived at the appointed hour and entered a lecture hall with too few seats. Hofferbert told the group,
sarcastically, that the Klan would not be there, and the presentation began. About fifteen minutes later, Hofferbert handed a
framed photo of his granddaughter at the Berlin Wall into the
crowd to pass around, and an African American student named
Marcello Tarry scornfully sent the photo sailing to the back of the
room, where it landed intact. Hofferbert and Tarry exchanged insults. Tarry tossed a wad of gum at Levin, and then placed a
soiled Kleenex in Hofferbert's coffee cup. Students around Tarry,
including the head of the Black Student Union, restrained him.

The four-minute dispute ended, Hofferbert finished his talk uninterrupted, a question-and-answer session followed in which members of the audience challenged the NAS for its stands on minority issues, and the session ended peaceably.

Right afterward, when Levin had his first chance to interpret the event, he low-keyed it. The student newspaper reporter on hand wrote that Levin was "surprised" at the strong reactions during the talk, but the paper added that "other than the one person who misbehaved, the meeting had gone well." An attending reporter for the local TV station decided the racial flare-up she'd been tipped off to hadn't panned out, and ran a story saying so that night.

But more than two weeks later, David Rossie, columnist for the *Binghamton Press & Sun-Bulletin*, wrote his version of the events he never witnessed, in which a cane- and club-wielding "mob" mimicked the tactics of "the Nazis' heyday," "Stalin's reign of terror," and "Mao's cultural revolution." Rossie demanded "strong measures to halt the university's decline into savagery." Similar wording appeared ten days later in the *Wall Street Journal* editorial, followed by slight variations in the *New York Post* under the headlines "Outrage at SUNY-Binghamton" and "The Brownshirts and the Cowards."

Where did they get their information? Not from the "mob," none of whom were quoted. The Rossie, *WSJ*, and *Post* versions most closely resemble a March 17 memo to college president Lois Defleur titled "Intimidation and Terrorism at NAS Lecture," written by NAS member Professor Michael C. Mittelstadt, who in addition called the local TV station in a rage over its low-key reporting of the episode. (Mittelstadt—lest one forget that on campuses much of the politics are internal—teaches with Levin in a classics department threatened with big cutbacks.) The memo was one of more than two dozen that NASers cranked out and sent to President Defleur right after the lecture, according to Professor Aldo Bernardo, founder of NAS's Binghamton chapter. When Defleur did not endorse the NAS horror story, it was time to blitz

Rossie and others in the media with the same correspondence.

Rossie, for his part, admits that "to a large extent" he relied on the NAS version of events, gleaned through interviews with NAS members. He didn't bother to call Santos, Rossie says, having decided ahead of time that "he's not credible."

WSJ editorial writer Dorothy Rabinowitz didn't call Santos or any of the other alleged "storm troopers," either. She did talk with Defleur, whose studied position was that the NASers had hyped the facts out of all proportion. But Rabinowitz ignored her findings and concentrated on Nazi imagery instead. Anyone who took President Defleur's view, she says, "has not a leg to stand on, because they refuse to see what happened. . . . They live in terror of being politically incorrect. So that's what it is and that's the explanation for everything."

I did some of the investigating and reporting that Rossie and Rabinowitz found inconvenient, interviewing student journalists who were at the lecture, reviewing a videotape and an audio recording of the event, and talking to all sides. I found:

• Gonzalo Santos, branded the "mob" instigator by the NAS and the local newspaper, was recorded telling a group of students before they entered the lecture hall that they should challenge the NAS "with our minds, with our arguments."

• Marcello Tarry was the only student who caused trouble, and the audience acted to police his behavior, *preventing* him from causing further commotion. Afterward, Tarry was disciplined and placed on probation, according to the NAS's Saul Levin. Still unsatisfied, Levin is formally demanding a ban on all "indoor demonstrations of any kind," and even "crowding into rooms."

• No one was hurt, no property destroyed, the entire lecture was delivered, the question-and-answer session was spirited but civil. The clubs supposedly brandished consisted of one walking stick used as such, and a handful of pledge canes carried as symbols of fraternity membership. No NAS member we interviewed claims that the stick or canes were ever raised or displayed in a threatening way.

Our findings jibe with a May 12 *Newsday* article by Ken Fireman, who reviewed the audio tape and talked to many witnesses, including an on-campus plainclothes officer, and reconstructed a "much less ominous picture of the incident" than the one presented by the NAS. Fireman showed that a single disrupter was used to brand an entire audience responsibly exercising its right to free speech as a "mob." Fireman's careful journalism, coming a month after the *WSJ* and *Post* versions, was too late to offset what the NAS, given its pedigree, must have considered a media coup.

That pedigree, as Sara Diamond has documented (see pp. 89-96), is profoundly and actively conservative. The four-year-old, fourteen-hundred-member NAS gets funding from prominent right-wing foundations, publishes a journal that attacks everything from feminist scholarship to supposed "leftist control" of Latin America, and is closely linked with what is now the Madison Center for Educational Affairs, begun by neocon guru Irving Kristol and former treasury secretary William Simon and founded under its present name by William Bennett and Allan Bloom. Another of the Madison Center's pet projects is the funding and promotion of dozens of conservative campus newspapers around the nation.

If you're a George Will wannabe, the Madison Center wants you! In fact, its Collegiate Network will send you *Start the Presses! A Handbook for Alternative Student Journalists*, to help you launch your own right-wing tabloid. In the copy I obtained, Midge Decter welcomes young PC-bashers to the "war of ideas," and asks: "Am I saying that you should be quite ideologically narrow? The answer is yes. . . . " *Start the Presses!* is chockablock with tips on how to sneak political hit pieces in between innocuous record reviews, develop spies, portray conservatives as embattled martyrs, and keep from melting when the heat is reflected back. If the Madison Center and its projects want to train guerrillas for Decter's "war of ideas," there is nothing too surprising in that, and its savvy political organizing might have something to teach the Left. But it's good to keep such things in mind the next time the NAS or some other anti-PC warriors argue, as they often do, that they are simply for depoliticizing academia.

Out of this milieu dedicated to portraying young Republicans as victims of oppression came Dinesh D'Souza, himself the editor of one of the most notorious campus con papers, the *Dartmouth Review*. "Distort D'Newza," as some Dartmouthers unfondly remember him, was on board when the paper published an interview with a former Ku Klux Klan leader, along with a staged photo of a black man hanging from a tree on the Dartmouth campus, and when it sponsored a free lobster-and-champagne meal to coincide with a campus fast against world hunger. In charge, D'Souza ran a supposed parody statement from a supposed affirmative-action candidate: "Now we be comin' to Dartmut and be up over our 'fros in studies, but we still be not graduatin' Phi Beta Kappa." Upon graduation, D'Souza went the way of other idealistic, "alternative" journalists who write what's unpopular, damn the consequences: he moved, via a short stint at the Heritage Foundation, into the Reagan administration as senior policy analyst focusing on domestic issues. Since 1988, he has been ensconced at the American Enterprise Institute, part of the cushy think-tank system that conservative money has built. In that world, chutzpah of Reaganesque proportion pays off; D'Souza decided to write a book in which he would seem to be handwringing over all the racial fuss on campus—which, of course, he had done his best to create.

When your politics can't promise change to those getting screwed by them, the best defense is a good offense: blame the inevitably resulting unrest on an enemy within by demonizing the dissidents. Thus, feminists, multiculturalists, and other challengers of entrenched power become "McCarthyites"—although the victims of McCarthy in the 1950s certainly didn't have national cover stories rushing to their defense. In a letter to the *Chronicle of Higher Education*, psychology professor Leon

Kamin, who during the McCarthy period was among dozens of academics fired or made unemployable for refusing to cooperate with congressional inquisitions, wrote: "It is difficult for me to take seriously the present bleating of D'Souza and the National Association of Scholars. I do not recall their predecessors voicing great concern about the 'political correctness' quite literally endorsed by state power. . . . "

That seemed a good point, so we tried to call George Will, who had struck a spark with his "thought police" allusion. Would he agree that, since then, demagogues on the Right had been busy labeling their opponents McCarthyites (and Nazi Stalinist Maoists) just because they smelled political opportunity? George Will was busy making speeches all over the country, so he probably couldn't call back for a five-minute conversation, his assistant told us. He didn't.

What Happened to English 306

■ ■ ■

LINDA BRODKEY
SHELLI FOWLER

■ ■ ■

I N T H E S P R I N G of 1990, a new syllabus was developed for
English 306, the writing requirement for entering students at
the University of Texas at Austin. But the course, Writing about
Difference, never made it to the classroom, becoming a casualty
of a disinformation campaign in which it was labeled by one professor as "the most massive attempt at thought-control ever attempted on the campus."

About 60 percent of first-year students at Austin take English
306, an expository writing class. As at most universities, the
class is taught almost exclusively by Ph.D. candidates in literary
studies. Over the past several years the course has received less
than favorable student evaluations. The graduate-student instructors say studying literature doesn't prepare them to design
and teach composition. They're right. (Their evaluations are dramatically better when they teach literature.) In their case, poor
teaching is a matter of poor teacher-preparation.

In the fall of 1989, the policy committee that oversees first-
and second-year English classes, made up of seven faculty and
two graduate students (including ourselves), set out to improve
English 306. By spring the committee determined that the
course, to be called Writing about Difference, would teach argumentation as critical inquiry, focusing on federal court opinions
dealing with discrimination in education and employment. Graduate students would teach from a common syllabus in the

1990–91 academic year and, thereafter, experienced instructors would be free to continue using the syllabus or to develop one of their own. Even though regular faculty rarely teach English 306 and all were exempted from using the common syllabus, 10 percent were excited enough by our plans that they volunteered to teach the syllabus.

In the late spring, an ad hoc committee was formed to develop the syllabus for Writing about Difference. Following guidelines set by the policy committee, we defined argumentation as critical inquiry. Federal court opinions we selected had at least three arguments (the plaintiff's, the defendant's, and the court's) and the goal was to teach students that an argument is not merely a debate between two sides, but that one might take any number of positions. Assignments for the course were designed to teach students critical inquiry as part of laying out a case for whatever position each has.

While we were planning Writing about Difference, opposition to the course was gathering on campus. We had completed a working draft of the syllabus by July 23, the day the dean of liberal arts announced his decision to postpone the class for a year, in order to address what he called "misunderstandings about the course expressed within the university community."

The "misunderstandings" did not have to do with the syllabus. Neither the dean nor those in "the university community" whose publicized opposition influenced his decision saw the syllabus until weeks after the course was postponed. That leaves us to conclude that opponents were concerned not about how we planned to teach writing but about the topic – difference. They projected their fears onto graduate-student teachers, who they claimed would force students to write what the media later came to call "PC" essays. Two members of the committee resigned. And on February 4, after six months of fending off criticism and trying to have the course field-tested in several sections, the policy committee resigned en bloc.

Not so long ago, colleagues who shared progressive beliefs occasionally described some of their actions as being "politically correct." The use of the term was invariably ironic. The Right's current appropriation, however, PC, is devoid both of the collegial tone and of the irony. On college campuses today, PC is a shibboleth for flushing out advocates of multicultural education. This is exactly what opponents of the course at Austin attempted to do, and, with a little help from the media, they were successful. "Good Riddance," a recent editorial in the *Houston Chronicle* crowing over the resignation of the committee, claims we were part of "a new McCarthyism" and "a new fascism of the left," and so gave just cause for routing the epigones of "latter-day versions of the Hitler Youth or Mao Tse-Tung's Red Guards." A course like Writing about Difference, the *Chronicle* assures readers, "is elitist cant masquerading as tolerance; it is, in short, an idea inimical to the concept of a university." No one could fault the *Houston Chronicle* for not defining what it means by PC. Though a good many at the University of Texas could take this and other publications to task for not knowing the difference between a course and a spin on a course.

Not one of the many journalists who have trotted out Writing about Difference as an example of the dangers of political correctness interviewed anyone who actually worked on the syllabus. Freedom from information (beyond the spin put on the course by its opponents) may explain why syndicated columnist George Will felt free to tack "Race and Gender" onto the course title; why Richard Bernstein reported in the *New York Times* that "literary classics" had to be dropped to make room for the PC materials; why *Newsweek* did not know in December that the leftist Rothenberg reader had been dropped in June; why Fred Siegel, writing for the *New Republic*, mistakenly claims that English 306 is a "remedial writing course" whose theme is "white male racism."

If they had spoken to us, we could have told Mr. Will that difference is an open category, which allowed us to select court cases dealing with disability, ethnicity, bilingualism, and sexual orientation, as well as race and gender; Bernstein would have learned that the cases didn't displace any literary classics (our liberal arts catalogue requires that English 306 use expository writing); *Newsweek* might have been surprised to hear that we dropped the Rothenberg book when we realized we weren't going to use enough of it to justify asking students to buy it. No one in the field of composition would mistake English 306 for a remedial writing course, and it's patently absurd to claim that federal laws and court opinions spell "white male racism."

Judging by the sheer number of times Writing about Difference appears in articles on PC, the spin undoubtedly makes good copy. But we find it alarming that opponents of the course were able to convince the press that students being required to analyze court opinions should be ridiculed for PC thinking. If learning to think and write critically about the arguments made and the issues raised in discrimination suits is labeled as "indoctrination" or "thought control" then we have to ask ourselves if opponents of this course are against critical thinking itself. At a time when students are complaining that teachers aren't interested in teaching, we must ask how courses such as Writing about Difference can even attempt to improve the quality of teaching if the press is also going to take the position that our motives are suspect.

Some of the most outspoken critics of Writing about Difference have been members of the National Association of Scholars. The NAS advocates courses it believes "transcend cultural differences," based on the assumption that "the truths of mathematics, the sciences, history, and so on, are not different for people of different races, sexes, or cultures." A good many people might say the NAS agenda is PC. But to do so misses the point. Its claim that truth transcends culture is arguable, as is ours that argument is contingent on critical inquiry. But serious intellectual differences about higher education cannot be resolved by accusing colleagues of being politically suspect. Opponents of our course and others like it may well believe we represent "a new McCarthyism of the Left," but surely the tactics they use to publicize their opposition (letters to local papers and to university donors) are those of the old McCarthyism.

When the *Austin-American Statesman* ran a letter last June from an English professor calling the course "the most massive attempt at thought-control ever attempted on the campus," the present of the University of Texas said nothing. When the dean of liberal arts postponed the revised course, the president still said nothing. But when the policy committee asked his permission to field-test the materials for the proposed course in selected sections, the president said no. Saying nothing is saying that the university believes Writing about Difference may be the PC course opponents claim it to be. But saying no to the duly appointed committee is saying no to academic freedom, which is why the *Houston Chronicle* should be worried rather than relieved by our resignation.

What Happened at Duke

■ ■ ■

NINA KING

■ ■ ■

ON PAPER, at least, it was a hot month in the curricular wars at Duke. The cover story of the March 1991 *Atlantic* magazine castigated prominent members of the English department for "radical skepticism," for an interpretive philosophy of "anything goes," and for lending political support to the left-leaning agendas of minority and feminist activists. A *New Republic* story portrayed department chairman Stanley Fish as a kind of would-be Nietzschean Superman, obsessed with power and the imposition of his own will. All month long editorialists, columnists, and letter-writers in the student newspaper, the *Chronicle*, fulminated about the imminent departure from Duke of Henry Louis Gates, famous scholar of Afro-American literature and infamous defender of the artistry of 2 Live Crew. Having flirted with Duke for three years before accepting its offer, "Skip" Gates was now leaving after a mere two years – and two courses – seduced by the siren song of Harvard. Then, in another headline development, Fish announced that he would step down as department chairman in December.

Meanwhile, in the classrooms of the Allen Building on Duke's neo-Gothic West Campus, it was business as usual.

• In English 145 (Milton), novelist Reynolds Price, as he has for twenty-three years, led forty or so students in animated discussions of *Paradise Lost*. The "greatest mystery of all" in the poem, said Price, is "the fact that Evil exists . . . and, if we assume the existence of a single Creator, that Evil derives at least in part from God." The students wrestled with this and other ancient conundrums – the nature of the Trinity, the puzzle of predestination. If their language was not always equal to the subject matter ("I was almost, like, gagging when Adam and Eve were fawning over each other," one young woman observed of Book IV), they were alert and intelligent, enthralled by Price's witty, passionate commentary.

• In Frank Lentricchia's English 170 (Studies in Genre), the theme was modernism, the method an experiment in co-teaching with Jodie McAuliffe from the drama department. Directed by McAuliffe, a small group of students gave a dramatic reading of a scene in Faulkner's story "Barn Burning." In the discussion that followed, Lentricchia focused on the interpretive problems faced, variously, by theatrical directors and literary critics and on the discovery of social class as a classic Faulknerian theme.

• In English 172 (Literary Theory), Barbara Herrnstein Smith, embarking on a survey of structuralist and poststructuralist theory, led her students in an exuberant deconstruction of the very notion of "literature" itself. The students clearly delighted in the daring of the exercise, though one remarked at class's end that in some earlier sessions, there had been even more "fireworks."

In the past five or six years, Duke's English department has become one of the most prestigious, and controversial, in the country. Starting in 1985, the administration, prodded by Lentricchia, hired a number of well-known professors who were on the cutting edge of critical theory or in the forefront of new specialties such as Afro-American and women's studies. Among them were theorists Fish and Smith; Gates; Jane Tompkins, a feminist expert in popular culture; and Fredric Jameson, a leading Marxist critic. Among the results: new English courses with titles like Melodrama and Soap Opera, Narcotics and Narrative, Colonialism and Neo-Colonialism in Fiction – viewed by some traditionalists as challenges to the classics of Western literature.

In the debates over the curriculum and over academic standards, literary theory has assumed an oddly prominent role—odd because of its fundamentally esoteric nature. Though a number of related theories are involved (poststructuralism, reader-response theory, postmodernism, new historicism, etc.), they often are lumped together under the ominous buzzword "deconstructionism." To oversimplify: the deconstructionists regard language as a tricky, slippery medium that cannot be pinned down to a single fixed meaning. The critic's task is to demonstrate that trickiness and slipperiness in a given work, to show how meaning changes shape when the medium is carefully examined. "Meaning" and, by extension, concepts such as "truth" and "art" are viewed as relative—historically and culturally determined rather than fixed for all time.

Critics of curricular innovation believe the radical relativism of deconstructionism gives rise to an "anything goes" attitude that undermines traditional hierarchical standards and makes Zora Neale Hurston or Toni Morrison or Louis L'Amour the equal of Shakespeare and Milton. (Not so, respond the deconstructionists; there are no absolute "standards" but each age, culture, or "interpretive community" arrives at its own.) The deconstructionists are also criticized for supporting the political agendas of leftist, minority, feminist, and homosexual activists. And all these groups are suspected of trying to indoctrinate students.

At Duke there has been posturing and intemperate outbursts on both sides. When a Duke chapter of the traditionalist National Association of Scholars was established, under the leadership of liberal political scientist James David Barber, Fish fired off a letter to the *Chronicle*, branding the group "racist, sexist and homophobic." In another now famous incident, Barber went to the political science section of the campus bookstore, pulled out all the books with "Marx" in their titles, and urged that they be removed from the shelves.

But if the proof of the pudding is in the pedagogy, Duke should be blessing its stars and superstars. During a month of eclectic attendance at courses in the English department, I was consistently impressed by the quality of the teaching: the spectacle of good teachers interacting with bright, well-prepared students, students who gave every indication of feeling free to speak their minds.

• In English 168 (Afro-American Literature), before turning to the day's assignment, Hurston's novel *Their Eyes Were Watching God*, Henry Louis Gates launched a discussion of the conflicts between black writers' responsibility to their race and to their art. It was an issue that struck home with some of the black students in the class, who clearly understood what James Baldwin meant by "the burden of representation" in this elite school where their numbers are few (some 400 of Duke's 6,000 undergraduates are black). Gates probed the students' reaction and suggested new angles; there was no political agenda in sight.

• In English 329, a graduate seminar, Stanley Fish took on Milton's *Areopagitica*. Though the new theorists are often portrayed as rejecting the canon, Fish's specialty is the ultra-canonical Milton. Reynolds Price, whose own Milton classes have been a Duke institution since 1968, describes him as "one of the leading Miltonists of the twentieth century."

To be sure, Fish's approach to Milton is far removed from that of the God-haunted Price. In Fish's rigorous rhetorical analysis, *Areopagitica*, traditionally regarded as a classic defense of a free press, became "a self-consuming artifact . . . a work which in a variety of ways invalidates itself." Not only did Fish demonstrate that Milton's devotion to free speech and a free press was severely limited, he also argued that Milton's view of truth had a good deal in common with the deconstructionists'. For Milton, imperfect man can only grasp at pieces of Truth; knowledge of the whole is deferred until Christ's Second Coming. For the deconstructionists, Fish noted, knowledge of the truth is also deferred. Eternally.

It was a bravura performance.

Surplus Visibility

■ ■ ■

KATHARINE T. BARTLETT

■ ■ ■

CRITICIZING CAMPUS "radicals" for browbeating the majority into some "politically correct" ideological conformity has become more fashionable than the practice it condemns. But the PC rap is a bum one. PC critics mischaracterize the enemy, exaggerate its presence, and fail to debate or even acknowledge the important substantive issues underlying the controversy. In doing so, they not only obscure, but also help to prove, the insights they themselves do not appear to understand.

The pejorative label "political correctness" represents an effort by PC critics to seize the moral high ground of the First Amendment. They claim that those protesting the continuation of racism and sexism on college campuses are moral ideologues, intolerant censors, Vietnam-protesters-turned-fascists. They also claim that these ideologues have taken over the universities, and that from this place of power they are threatening the quality of academic standards and the integrity of free intellectual inquiry.

Where is this ideological coercion? Where is this threat to open dialogue? I see little evidence of it, even at Duke University, which has been cited as a hotbed of PC. At Duke, courses on Shakespeare, Milton, and other "traditional" liberal arts subjects are not under siege; courses on such subjects as Marxism, women's studies, and Afro-American literature are. The average female Duke student shuns the label "feminist." In contrast, no shame appears to attach to association with conservative causes. Outspoken conservative students have their own newspaper, the

Duke Review, and an active chapter of the National Association of Scholars speaks freely. At Duke, academic traditionalists head almost all departments and hold almost all chaired professorships. Duke has only one female dean; all other top leadership positions are held by white men.

If Duke is typical, what accounts for the perception that university radicals have taken over? "Surplus visibility," answers Daphne Patai of the University of Massachusetts at Amherst. Certain voices are being heard in the university more often, more loudly, and more insistently than in the past. Given what we are accustomed to hearing from these voices — silence — the noise is deafening. As Ms. Patai observes, when members of groups we do not expect to hear from begin to speak, their voices appear too loud, out of place, inappropriate, excessive.

Surplus visibility exemplifies a larger phenomenon PC critics have been unwilling to understand: the privilege of those who have power to say what needs defending and what does not. In any social organization, the views of the dominant tend to be taken for granted as objective and neutral. Challenges to these views — like those we are now hearing in the universities — appear to seek special favors for the "less qualified," or some compromising of academic standards.

This phenomenon helps to explain why some demands pressed at universities are viewed as "political" or "special pleadings," while others are not. Some PC critics dismiss as interest-group politics requests that authors such as Toni Morrison or Mary Wollstonecraft be included in the curriculum; others malign courses in feminist theory or black studies as a "Balkanization" of the curriculum.

In contrast, assignments of writings by Nathaniel Hawthorne or T.S. Eliot draw no notice and require no defense; neither does the "basic" political philosophy course that begins with Aristotle and ends with John Rawls. The difference is *not* that the standard "Western civilization" courses are apolitical. In fact, it is precisely the alignment of these courses with particular points of view—the dominant ones in our society—that makes them appear neutral. This is not to argue that such courses should be abolished, but nobody should pretend that only feminist and minority-studies courses have political content.

PC critics attack as ideologically coercive, condescending, and petty the insistence by some "blacks" and "Indians" that they be called "African Americans" or "native Americans." Yet they take for granted their own titles of "Professor," "Doctor," or "Judge" as a matter of simple civility.

Most, perhaps all, titles and labels convey substantive political messages about power and self-definition. But those that conform to existing lines of authority are taken as neutral signs of respect, while those that implicitly encroach upon that authority stand out as shamelessly political and arrogant.

It is clear that some PC critics are using a double standard to judge those who do not respect their authority. These critics invoke important principles of academic freedom to shield themselves from criticism of classroom remarks that some students find racist or sexist. Yet they appear to acknowledge no reciprocal freedom on the part of students to resist classroom humiliation; and it is that resistance that is now labeled a "politically correct" effort at censorship.

Most of us who have been labeled PC are not seeking special favors. We are not trying to stifle debate. We are trying to begin one—a difficult one that challenges perspectives that are taken for granted in the university and in society. If our critics were true to the free-speech principles they profess, they would be engaging in that debate. All too often, they have chosen personal denunciation and caricature instead.

There is room, and a great need, for a genuine debate in our universities about academic quality and diversity. PC critics have diverted the debate by the distracting assertion, backed by only a few isolated anecdotes, that traditional voices are being silenced.

The one-sidedness of the PC critique mocks this assertion. It also demonstrates a central paradox of the whole PC problem: The more established the status quo, the less defense it requires, and the more easily challenges to it can be made to appear self-serving and tyrannical. The PC charge is a smoke screen. The fact that it packs rhetorical punch demonstrates that there has been far less change in who controls the university, and in what we take for granted there, than many would have us believe.

III

"IN MY

EXPERIENCE..."

■ ■ ■

What Revolution at Stanford?

■ ■ ■

RAOUL V. MOWATT

■ ■ ■

A S A N Y lover of Western culture could tell you, a rose by any other name would smell as sweet. Unless, of course, the rose were a Stanford University program once called "Western Culture." Then intellectuals and journalists would claim that civilization as we know it has come to an end with the program's rechristening as "Culture, Ideas, and Values."

Stanford altered its Western Culture requirement in March 1988, reacting to charges of intellectual bias against women and minorities. After two years of debate, the Faculty Senate abandoned the core list of fifteen required works to allow instructors greater flexibility in choosing texts. It also required increased emphasis on the works of women and people of color. Gone was Western Culture; in its place, Stanford would offer Cultures, Ideas, and Values, or CIV.

All hell broke loose.

Commentators off and on campus seemed compelled to give their views on the subject. Columnist Charles Krauthammer and author Allan Bloom denounced the change as pseudointellectual and trendy, while the Rev. Jesse Jackson and others claimed that Stanford students had won a great victory for multicultural education.

Both these positions were off the mark. In reality, if Bloom and Jackson were both to pore over the reading lists for the CIV courses, Bloom would have cause for a much greater degree of satisfaction.

For nearly three of my four years at Stanford I have been involved in one of the Western Culture/CIV tracks. As a freshman I was enrolled in Structured Liberal Education, or SLE, a Western Culture track that surveys Western art, literature, and philosophy, while the class was still under the auspices of the Western Culture program; as a junior and senior, I have been a writing tutor for the same course, which is now part of the CIV curriculum.

All this time I've been puzzled about how a debate on an academic decision could be so dominated by a lack of information. What follows is a sampling of the most common misconceptions about the Western Culture program:

Stanford formerly required all freshmen to take a single Western Culture course.

Actually, Stanford offered incoming students the choice of enrolling in one of eight yearlong sequences or tracks. Each had a slightly different emphasis; while one course examined the relationship between technology and ideas, for instance, another explored the development of philosophy.

Seven of those courses continue to be taught essentially as they were before. The change to CIV has led to the creation of one new track, "Europe and the Americas," which highlights intellectual developments that resulted from the discovery of the New World.

As a result of the switch to CIV, freshmen no longer read the great works of Western culture; instead they read such authors as Frantz Fanon, a black radical who advocated the mass murder of whites.

A trip to the Stanford Bookstore quickly gives the lie to this assertion. Last year, all eight tracks included selections from the Bible, Freud, Shakespeare, Aristotle, and St. Augustine. Six read Plato, Machiavelli, and Aquinas; by contrast, only two read Fanon and Confucius.

Besides wrongly reducing the situation to a zero-sum game, this claim ignores the logistics of most CIV courses, which are organized chronologically by quarter. Under this framework, modern authors compete for space solely with other modern authors, enabling students to become familiar with both the classics they need as background and the contemporary writings that interest them.

The only track that is ordered differently, Europe and the Americas, has an enrollment of about 50 out of about 1,500 freshmen – hardly representative of the program as a whole. Even here, students encounter numerous works from the canon.

The change to CIV meant a sweeping advance in multicultural education.

With the exception of the Europe and the Americas track, CIV continues to focus on white male Western culture, with a tip of the hat to such black writers as Ralph Ellison and Toni Morrison. Many of the tracks now teaching those authors were teaching them before.

The change to CIV was an attempt to indoctrinate freshmen with leftist ideology.

As a freshman in SLE I read Freud and Fanon, Machiavelli and Malcolm X, Rousseau and Adrienne Rich. I found all of them valuable to my intellectual development. Because of SLE, I have been alternately bored, stressed, and stimulated. I have written and read, argued and conceded many points about Western culture.

I have never fully understood the notion that faculty could brainwash me into believing whatever they wanted me to. As surveys of numerous works, thoughts, and paradigms, CIV courses pose little threat of indoctrination. Instead, they serve to introduce students to perspectives different from their own.

I took SLE side by side with students from all points of the ideological compass: Jews and born-again Christians, Muslims and Sikhs, leftists and rightists, black straights and white gays. The course was residentially based, which meant we frequently discussed Dante over dinner and consoled each other before papers were due. And most of the students I knew would claim that the course had changed how they thought, rather than what they thought. Reading Hitler did not make me a fascist; reading Sartre did not make me an existentialist. Both simply enabled me to think about those philosophies in ways I hadn't previously.

When I visit the students I tutor, I find that little has changed in this regard. Each academic quarter, I assist three students with their essays. Whether they amaze me with their innovative interpretations of a given text or disappoint me because they haven't thought sufficiently about their topic, I act as devil's advocate, mentor, and friend.

I do not mean to suggest that there is absolutely no difference at all between CIV now and Western Culture then. Indeed, it would be impossible for a campus to experience the sort of debate that Stanford did without some sort of change taking place. I remember watching the marchers rallying for CIV, chanting "Hey, Hey! Ho, Ho! Western Culture's gotta go!" I thought to myself, "So this is what it feels like to be in the midst of a revolution." I remember how a real sense of paranoia swept the campus after the Faculty Senate made its controversial decision. Many feared that an eccentric few had jeopardized the university's reputation; certainly there was a loss of self-esteem.

A steady stream of letters in the *Stanford Daily* mirrored the divisions on campus. People began to align themselves with one camp of "thought" or another, according to their perceptions of whether the course would worsen or alleviate racial tensions; few asked whether it would teach critical thinking.

Although most students now consider the issue dead and buried, the vestiges of those unnecessarily polarized camps still remain, and they still don't talk to each other rationally. The same holds true for the outside world.

What Campus Radicals?

■ ■ ■

ROSA EHRENREICH

■ ■ ■

A NATIONAL SURVEY of college administrators found
that "political correctness" is not the campus issue it has
been portrayed to be by pundits and politicians of the political
right. During the 1990–91 academic year, according to the survey's findings, faculty members complained of pressure from students and fellow professors to alter the political and cultural
content of their courses at only *5 percent* of all colleges. So much
for the influence of the radicals, tenured or otherwise.

The survey's findings came as no real surprise to me. The hegemony of the "politically correct" is not a problem at Harvard,
where I've just completed my undergraduate education, or at any
other campus I visited during my student years. But then none
among those who have escalated the PC debate in the past
year—Dinesh D'Souza and Roger Kimball, George Will and
George Bush, *Time* and *New York* magazines—is actually interested in what is happening on the campuses. In all the articles
and op-ed pieces published on PC, multiculturalism, etc., very
few student voices have been heard. To be a liberal arts student
with progressive politics today is at once to be at the center of a
raging national debate and to be completely on the sidelines,
watching others far from campus describe you and use you for
their own ends.

For instance: During the spring semester of my freshman year
at Harvard, Stephan Thernstrom, an American history professor,
was criticized by several black students for making "racially in-

sensitive" comments during lectures. The incident made the *Harvard Crimson* for a few days, then blew over after a week or so and was quickly forgotten by most students. It continued a kind of mythic afterlife, however, in the PC debate. Here is how it was described in a January 1991 *New York* magazine cover story by John Taylor on, in the author's words, the "moonies in the classroom" propagating the "new fundamentalism":

> "Racist." "Racist!" "The man is a racist!" "A *racist!*"
> Such denunciations, hissed in tones of self-righteousness and contempt, vicious and vengeful, furious, smoking with hatred – such denunciations haunted Stephan Thernstrom for weeks. Whenever he walked through the campus that spring, down Harvard's brick paths, under the arched gates, past the fluttering elms, he found it hard not to imagine the pointing fingers, the whispers.

The operative word here is "imagine." Taylor seriously distorted what actually happened. In February of 1988, several black female students told classmates that they had been disturbed by some "racially insensitive" comments made by Professor Thernstrom. Thernstrom, they said, had spoken approvingly of Jim Crow laws, and had said that black men, harboring feelings of inadequacy, beat their female partners. The students, fearing for their grades should they anger Professor Thernstrom by confronting him with their criticisms – this is not an unusual way for college students to think things through, as anyone who's been an undergraduate well knows – never discussed the matter with him. They told friends, who told friends, and the *Crimson* soon picked up word of the incident and ran an article.

Professor Thernstrom, understandably disturbed to learn of the matter in the *Crimson*, wrote a letter protesting that no students had ever approached him directly with such criticisms. He also complained that the students' vague criticisms about "racial insensitivity" had "launched a witch-hunt" that would have "chilling effect[s] upon freedom of expression." Suddenly, Professor Thernstrom was to be understood as a victim, falsely smeared with the charge of racism. But no one had ever accused him of any such thing. "I do not charge that [Thernstrom] is a racist," Wendi Grantham, one of the students who criticized Thernstrom, wrote to the *Crimson* in response to his letter. Grantham believed the professor gave "an incomplete and over-simplistic presentation of the information. . . . I am not judging [his] character; I am simply asking questions about his presentation of the material. . . . " As for the professor's comment that the criticisms were like a "witch-hunt," Grantham protested that Thernstrom had "turned the whole situation full circle, proclaimed himself victim, and resorted to childish name-calling and irrational comparisons. . . 'witch-hunt' [is] more than a little extreme. . . . " But vehement, even hysterical language is more and more used to demonize students who question and comment. Terms like *authoritarian* and *Hitler youth* have been hurled at students who, like Grantham, dare to express any sort of criticism of the classroom status quo.

In my four years as a student at Harvard, I found few signs of a new fascism of the Left. For that matter, there are few signs of the Left at all. The Harvard-Radcliffe Democratic Socialists Club collapsed due to lack of members, as did the left-wing newspaper the *Subterranean Review*. As to the neoconservative charge that the traditional political left has been supplanted by a feminist-gay-multicultural left: In my senior year the African-American Studies department and the Women's Studies committee each had so few faculty that the same woman served as chair of both. I got through thirty-two courses at Harvard, majoring in the history and literature of England and America, without ever being required to read a work by a black woman writer, and of my thirty-two professors only two were women. I never even *saw* a black or Hispanic professor. (Fewer than 10 percent of tenured professors at Harvard are women, and fewer than 7 percent are members of minorities.)

Perhaps, as some conservatives have maintained, even a few

radical professors can reach hundreds of students, bending their minds and sending them, angry and politicized, out into society upon graduation. To cure such fears, drop by Harvard's Office of Career Services. Most staffers there spend their days advising those who would be corporate execs, financial consultants, and investment bankers. Nearly 20 percent of the class of 1990 planned to go to law school. This compares with 10 percent who claimed that they would eventually go into government or one of what Career Services calls the "helping professions."

President Bush, speaking at the University of Michigan's 1991 commencement exercises, went on about radical extremists on campus. It would be interesting to know how he calculated this rise in radicalism. Two thirds of Harvard students wholeheartedly supported the Gulf War, according to one *Crimson* poll. That's more support for the war than was found in the country at large. And during my years at Harvard I found that most women on campus, including those who consider themselves politically liberal, would not willingly identify themselves as feminists.

The very notion of "politicization" makes most Harvard students nervous. I discovered this in the fall of 1989, when I was elected president of Harvard's community service organization, Phillips Brooks House Association. I had been reckless enough to suggest that volunteers would benefit from having some awareness of the social and political issues that affected the communities in which they did their volunteer work. I was promptly attacked in the *Crimson* for trying to inappropriately "politicize" public service. The paper also suggested that under my leadership volunteer training might mimic a "party line," with Brooks House as a "central planning office." This used to be called redbaiting. (So much for the liberal campus media.)

Meanwhile—and unremarked upon by D'Souza, et al.—the campus right thrives nationally. Two new right-wing vehicles have popped up on Harvard's campus in recent years. The Association Against Learning in the Absence of Religion and Morality

(AALARM) initially made a splash with its uninhibited gay-bashing. The magazine *Peninsula*, closely tied to AALARM, bears an uncanny editorial resemblance to the notorious *Dartmouth Review*, claims to uphold Truth, and has a bizarre propensity for centerfold spreads of mangled fetuses. And older, more traditional conservative groups have grown stronger and more ideological. The Harvard Republican Club, once a stodgy and relatively inactive group, suffered a rash of purges and resignations as more moderate members were driven out by the far right. It is inactive no more.

There *are* those on the Left who are intolerant and who could stand to lighten up a bit – these are the activists whom *progressive* and *liberal* students mockingly called "politically correct" years before the Right appropriated the term, with a typical lack of irony. But on the whole, intolerance at Harvard – and, I suspect, elsewhere – is the province mostly of extreme conservatism. Posters put up at Harvard by the Bisexual, Gay and Lesbian Students Association are routinely torn down. I don't recall any Republican Club posters being ripped up or removed.

The day after the bombing started in Iraq, I went to an event advertised as "a nonpartisan rally to support our troops," sponsored by the Republican Club. After the scheduled speakers – and several other nonscheduled speakers – had finished, I tried to speak. The rally organizers promptly turned off the microphone. I kept speaking, saying that I supported the troops but not the war. I added that I had been disturbed to hear it said by rally organizers – and applauded by the audience – that the time for debate was over. In a democracy, I said, the time for debate is never over.

I would have gone on, but at this point a group of men in the audience felt the need to demonstrate their conviction that there should be no debate. They began to loudly chant "victory" over and over, quite effectively drowning me out. By way of contrast, supporters of the war were listened to in polite silence by the crowd at an antiwar rally the next day.

In the classroom, too, right-wing political views are heard without disruption. One of Harvard's largest core courses, taken by nearly half of all undergraduates while I was there, is Social Analysis 10, Principles of Economics. It was taught, during my undergrad years, by two of President Reagan's top economic advisers, Martin Feldstein and Larry Lindsay. Students did not rise up *en masse* to protest the course's right-wing political bias; instead, they sat scribbling feverishly in their notebooks: Ec-10 had a notoriously steep grading curve. (No one seemed worried that each year some 750 innocent Harvard students were being lectured to by the engineers of what George Bush, in one of his more forthright moments, once referred to as "voodoo economics.")

There are many other politically conservative professors at Harvard whose courses are quite popular—Richard Pipes on Russian history and Samuel P. Huntington on modern democracy, to name two of the most prominent—and in their classrooms, as in all undergrad classrooms I was in, free and open discussion did quite well. I took many classes in which fearless conservatives rushed to take part in entirely civil discussions about the efficacy and justice of affirmative action, about whether books like *Uncle Tom's Cabin* and Frederick Douglass's autobiography are "really *literature*," as opposed to just interesting historical documents, and about whether it's at all fair or even interesting to condemn Jefferson for owning slaves even as he decried slavery. These are all valid questions, and all sides deserve a hearing—which, in my experience, is exactly what they always got.

And my experience was not unique. Most other Harvard students seemed to agree that there's no such thing as a cadre of PC thought police. Last winter the Republican Club laid huge sheets of poster board across several dining-hall tables and put up a sign asking students to scribble down their responses to the question "Is there free speech at Harvard?" The vast majority of students wrote things like "What's the big deal? Of course there's free speech here." And the lively, cheerful discussion going on among the students gathered around the tables attested to that fact.

Conservatives like D'Souza and Kimball charge that traditional Western culture courses barely exist anymore at schools like Harvard, because of some mysterious combination of student pressure and the multiculturalist, post-structuralist tendencies of radical professors. Writing in the *Atlantic*, Caleb Nelson, a former editor of the conservative *Harvard Salient*, complained that in the 1989–90 Harvard course catalogue

> no core Literature and Arts course lists any of the great nineteenth-century British novelists among the authors studied, nor does any list such writers as Virgil, Milton, and Dostoevsky. In the core's history areas even students who . . . took every single course would not focus on any Western history before the Middle Ages, nor would they study the history of the Enlightenment, the Renaissance, the American Civil War, or a host of other topics that one might expect a core to cover.

Nelson's major complaint is that Harvard is not properly educating all of its students. I agree with him here; in Caleb Nelson, Harvard has let us all down by producing a student so poorly educated that he's unable even to read the course catalogue.

I have the 1989–90 catalogue in front of me as I write, and a quick sampling of some of the entries gives us, from the Literature and Arts and the Historical Study sections of the core curriculum, the following courses: Chaucer, Shakespeare, The Bible and Its Interpreters, Classical Greek Literature and Fifth-Century Athens, The Rome of Augustus, The British Empire, The Crusades, The Protestant Reformation. Perhaps Chaucer and Shakespeare are somehow, to Caleb Nelson, not "such writers" as Milton and Dostoevsky and the Protestant Reformation is a historically trivial topic.

Nelson also worries that students will have "no broad look at . . . philosophy"—by which he really means Western philosophy. Yet in the Moral Reasoning section of the core, seven of the ten courses listed have at least four of the following authors on their primary reading lists: Plato, Aristotle, Thucydides, Machiavelli, Locke, Kant, Rousseau, Hume, Mill, Nietzsche, Marx, and Weber. There is one course devoted to a non-Western philosopher: Confucius. The remaining two Moral Reasoning courses focus, respectively, on the writings of "Aristotle . . . [and] Maimonides," and of "Jesus as presented in the Gospels."

These courses are far more representative of those taken by most Harvard undergraduates than the titillating and much denounced 1991 English course on Cross-Dressing and Cultural Anxiety—a graduate seminar listed in the course catalogue but ultimately never held. But then, if you are a right-winger looking for something to replace the commies on campus—remember them?—you aren't going to sell books or raise funds or win votes complaining about undergrads studying Confucian Humanism and Moral Community.

Many of the loudest complainers about PC thought police are those who are doing their best to curb free expression in other areas. It doesn't appear to bother Dinesh D'Souza that the word "abortion" cannot be uttered at a federally funded family clinic. More broadly, the brouhaha about political conformity on campus serves as a perfect smoke screen, masking from Americans—from ourselves—the rigid political conformity *off* campus: the blandness of our political discourse, the chronic silence in Washington on domestic matters, the same faces returned to office each year, the bipartisanship that keeps problems from becoming issues. During the Gulf War, the number of huge yellow bouquets in public places rivaled the number of larger-than-life photos of Saddam Hussein displayed on Iraqi billboards. Patriotically correct.

The campuses are no more under siege by radicals than is the society at large. It has been clever of the Kimballs and D'Souzas to write as if it were so. It is always clever of those in ascendance to masquerade as victims. Rebecca Walkowitz, the newly elected president of the *Harvard Crimson*, understands perfectly how this dynamic works. Referring to the 1988 incident involving Professor Thernstrom and several of his black students, Walkowitz has said: "People call the *Crimson* and ask what we 'did to that man.' It's important to remember who has the power here, because it's not students. Who would dare criticize a professor for political reasons now? In addition to fearing for your grade, you'd fear being pilloried in the national press."

Politically Correct Is Politically Suspect

■ ■ ■

MILES HARVEY

■ ■ ■

G EORGE BUSH USED his May 4, 1991, University of Michigan commencement address to denounce the "Orwellian" advocates of political correctness at the nation's colleges. American learning institutions, the president warned, were being endangered by a PC ethic that "declares certain topics off-limits, certain expressions off-limits, even certain gestures off-limits." Comparing political correctness to an "inquisition," Bush then proudly praised the "freedom to speak one's mind."

I happened to be at that graduation ceremony – receiving my master's degree – and what the president said made me furious.

On the one hand, I was mad because I knew that this suddenly pious defender of free speech was the same man who had baited Michael Dukakis as a "card-carrying member of the American Civil Liberties Union." On the other hand, I was angry because I could not deny that George Bush was right. No matter how hypocritical, hollow, and demagogic, the president's assertion that "on the 200th anniversary of the Bill of Rights, we find free speech under attack . . . on some college campuses" was, by my own observation, more than a little true.

True, George Bush and other conservatives use the PC issue for their own slimy political ends. But does this mean that they fabricated the issue out of thin air?

It would be comforting to think so. Yet listening to Bush that morning in Ann Arbor, I couldn't help but recall a meeting I had attended on campus a few months earlier. It was a gathering of graduate students who taught undergraduate creative writing courses. We were there to talk pedagogy. The conversation was predictably forgettable until the topic turned to sexism. It was then that one of my fellow teachers announced that she had established a rule for her students: Men were not allowed to write about rape in their short stories or poems.

My colleague's gag law was apparently based on two assumptions—first, that men would write about the subject only to indulge their own sexual fantasies, and second, that exploring such fantasies on paper is inherently a bad thing, somehow akin to the act itself. While I otherwise greatly respected my associate, her logic here reminded me of Jesse Helms's contention that exhibiting Robert Mapplethorpe's homoerotic photographs would somehow pose a threat to the American family. I was shocked when others at the meeting voiced their approval of my co-worker's approach. They constituted only a vocal minority, perhaps, but a very disturbing one—especially given the fact that all were writers themselves, and thus potential targets of the same kind of censorship.

A lone anecdote such as this, of course, proves nothing. Yet there were many others, and a few institutional examples of PC as well. In 1989, the year I entered graduate school at Michigan, the courts declared unconstitutional sections of the university's student-discipline policy. That policy prohibited "any behavior, *verbal* or physical [emphasis added], that stigmatizes or victimizes an individual on the basis of race, ethnicity, religion, sex, sexual orientation, creed, national origin, ancestry, age, marital status, handicap, or Vietnam-era veteran status."

Behind this rule is an idea, long cherished by conservatives like Helms, but lately appropriated by some on the Left. In essence, it is this: the rights of those offended by what someone says outweigh the rights of the person who says it. The University of Michigan was hardly alone in adopting this approach. Brown University, for example, recently expelled a student who shouted racist slurs. The University of Connecticut attempted to kick a student out of university housing for a similar offense. And there are many other examples from schools around the country.

I am not in any way trying to dismiss the very real problems of rape and racism, both of which are terrifyingly prevalent on university campuses today. Nor am I endorsing the right-wing position that political correctness constitutes a "New McCarthyism," in which universities are academic gulags run by tyrannical "thought police" who stifle all freedom of expression. (Many of those espousing this "New McCarthyism" line are, in fact, Old McCarthyites.)

What I *am* saying is that during my two years at graduate school, I perceived a kind of general free-speech funk, a faint but undeniable stench of intolerance in the hallowed halls. Despite reports to the contrary, American democracy will survive this ill wind – and so, for better or worse, will the cherished institution of academic debate. Bickering about trivial things, after all, is what keeps scholars busy.

But I would also argue that political correctness is counterproductive; that it actually *contributes* to the problems (sexism, rape, racism, homophobia) it sets out to correct; and that people on the Left should resist the temptation to be PC, not only because of abstract concepts like freedom of speech, but for practical political reasons as well.

There are a lot of complex theories about how PCness came to alight on American universities. I don't have the space to explore them but I will offer one obvious explanation. As with all workplaces, institutions of higher learning demand ever-increasing specialization from their employees. The way a scholar gets to the top these days is to find a tiny niche of expertise early in his or her career, then stick with it.

In the humanities, many such niches are often in the area of criticism, which is itself an inherently political endeavor. Universities are filled with Marxist scholars, feminist scholars, deconstructionist scholars, etc. These people have not only an ideological stake in promoting a specific political point of view, but an economic one as well. Many professors still give lip service to the admirable old concept that the purpose of higher education is to teach students *how* to think, not *what* to think. But they all know that generalists wind up on community-college staffs: it's the *what* that earns tenure.

There are other motivations. Many of my colleagues would speak of the desire to "wake up" their students – and I could hardly blame them for this impulse. I taught a news-writing class in which I was amazed to discover that few of my students regularly read a daily paper. Today's undergraduates, I realized, grew up almost entirely in the Reagan era. Many of them have adopted its values, showing little interest in anything outside their own lives. They are conservative by default. As University of Michigan undergraduate Andrew Gottesman, writing in the *Chicago Tribune*, explained: "I'm not going to attack or defend PC, mostly because I, like most other college students, have better things to do with my time. Like go to a bar. Watch a ballgame. Make a friend. Sleep."

Sen. Bill Bradley (Dem.-N.J.), decrying the horrid state of racial relations in this country, made an eloquent appeal for Americans to engage in an "honest dialogue" about the issue. "The more Americans are honest about the level of distrust they hold for each other," Bradley argued, "the easier it will be to get beyond those feelings and forge a new relationship without racial overtones."

I agree with the senator wholeheartedly, but wonder if this "honest dialogue" is now feasible. When Bradley made his plea in July 1991, I was in the process of reading some William Faulkner novels. I was amazed by Faulkner's head-on, unflinching treatment of skin color. His characters, black and white, are often at the same time victims of racism and racists themselves. Faulkner explores racial relations in all their complexity, never reducing them to safe simplifications.

I doubt I will ever find the courage to deal with race so forthrightly in my own prose. But if Faulkner were alive today, would he still be so bold? His books remind me oddly of Spike Lee's films. Like Faulkner, Lee does not try to make tidy observations about race; his work is full of perilous ambiguity. Because of it, Lee has been steadily pasted with labels of political indecorum that, accurate or not, are all too easily applied. I suspect that countless writers, artists, musicians, and filmmakers now shy away — perhaps subconsciously — from dangerous work that might get them branded racist, sexist, misogynist.

How about *lookist*? That's the word some staff members at Smith College used when warning their students not to judge people by their physical attractiveness. Or *ableist*, the Smith term for prejudice against the *differently abled* — itself a PC expression for handicapped.

Then there's *laughism*, a University of Connecticut word for inappropriate responses to ethnic jokes and other un-PC snickering. It's no wonder students seem so grim these days. Robert Schmuhl, who teaches American humor at the University of Notre Dame, recently noted "a growing reluctance to respond to humor in the public setting of the classroom out of fear that any exercise of one's funny bone will be misinterpreted."

But outside the classroom, he discovered, it's a different story. In a *Chicago Tribune* essay, Schmuhl reported that many of his students privately confess to finding hate-driven humorists like Andrew Dice Clay and Sam Kinison uproariously funny. "Students today are caught in a crossfire of competing cultural movements," he concluded. "One force (principally the academic establishment) pulls them in the direction of sensitivity. The other force (largely popular culture) jerks them toward the shocking or sensational. There's no middle ground."

I'm not sure it's very different for the rest of the country. Senator Bradley seems to be searching for just such a "middle ground" on the issue of race. And with good reason. Don't Andrew Dice Clay and David Duke share a constituency of people who might never say the word *nigger* but nonetheless think it every time they encounter an African American? And didn't the Clarence Thomas confirmation hearings demonstrate a similarly frightening polarity on topics of gender?

Other issues—from homophobia to xenophobia—also demand a frank national dialogue. But is honest discussion of such issues possible if the ground rules are that no one can be offended? And if Ronald Reagan's insistence on calling missiles "peacekeepers" polluted the arms-control debate, doesn't similarly abstract (albeit PC) language endanger exchanges about dozens of other pressing topics?

The PC push is not only hampering free speech and inquiry, it has also proven grossly ineffective. It's time for the Left—on campus and off—to stop trying to force our ideas on others. We must return to the business of listening, arguing, convincing. This is the true political correctness.

Political Correctness and
Identity Politics

■ ■ ■

BARBARA EPSTEIN

■ ■ ■

I HESITATE TO TAKE the term "political correctness" out of
quotation marks because I have never heard it used on the
Left except in a joking way; as far as I know it is not used to refer to
a politics that anyone actually endorses. Also, I hesitate to adopt
a term that carries the right-wing agenda of the neoconservatives.
But the term does get at what seems to me to be a troubling atmosphere on the Left, having to do with the intersection of identity
politics and moralism. The neoconservatives describe "politically correct" students and faculty denouncing and intimidating liberals, and clearly there are instances of this – but what I am more
aware of is a process of self-intimidation in the name of sensitivity
to racism, sexism, and homophobia, which tends to close down
discussion and make communication more difficult. John Taylor,
in his article on PC in *New York* magazine, claims that the guiding
principle of PC is "Watch what you say."[1] People are being denounced, he writes, for speaking of Indians rather than native
Americans or blacks rather than African Americans, or for using
the word *girl* rather than *woman* – even when the person in question is a teenager. One can object that we *should* watch what we

1. John Taylor, "Are You Politically Correct?" *New York*, January 21, 1991.
On p. 37, Taylor says that "making people watch what they say is the central
preoccupation of politically correct students."

say: that this is what is required to criticize, and ideally transform, a culture that is deeply imbued with racism, sexism, and
homophobia. Still, there is a difference between maintaining a
critical awareness of the assumptions behind our language and
creating a subculture in which everyone is on edge, waiting to be
charged with bias or looking for opportunities to accuse others
of it.

I frequently find myself in discussions that seem to be dominated by a collective fear of saying something wrong: fear of
betraying a racist, sexist, or homophobic attitude, or criticizing a
movement made up of women, people of color, or homosexuals. I
find this atmosphere of self-intimidation among students, among
faculty, and in progressive circles outside the university. A few
examples: I teach in the History of Consciousness Board at the
University of California at Santa Cruz. For years I have used
Clayborne Carson's book, *In Struggle: SNCC and the Black
Awakening of the 1960s,*[2] in my course on social movements. It
has become more and more difficult for me to induce what are always predominantly white classes to discuss this book, which
asks how SNCC moved from a nonviolent politics with a broad appeal to a more sectarian politics with a much narrower base. The
students read it, I can tell from their papers that they learn from
it, but discussion is halting at best. The last time this happened
students acknowledged—under my prodding—that they could
not talk about the book without entertaining criticisms of a black
movement, which would raise the possibility of racism.

I have also had a hard time, though of a different sort, with discussions of Alice Echols's *Daring to Be Bad: Radical Feminism
in America, 1967–1975,*[3] an account of radical feminism in the
late sixties and early seventies, which includes accounts of the
ideological rigidities and personal attacks that took place under

2. Clayborne Carson, *In Struggle: SNCC and the Black Awakening of the 1960s*
(Cambridge: Harvard University Press, 1981).
3. Alice Echols, *Daring to Be Bad: Radical Feminism in America, 1967–1975*
(Minneapolis: University of Minnesota Press, 1989).

the slogan of "the personal is political." Echols's book is dedicated to the goals of radical feminism, just as Carson's is to the goals of the civil rights movement. But both books include candid accounts of problems. My class, which was predominantly female and strongly feminist, was not silenced by this book, but the tone of the discussion was disapproving. Students' comments implied that an account that placed women, especially feminists, in a bad light was sexist. Some students argued that even if early feminists had made some mistakes, to write about them was to give ammunition to the enemy.

This kind of attitude is by no means limited to students. I attended a meeting of feminists of my own generation – some academics, some activists – held to discuss Echols's book. Most of the women who had not been directly involved in this history (which in this case mostly meant the women more identified with academia) argued that Echols must be wrong, that these things could not have happened, that if they had happened surely they had not been very important and should not be emphasized in an account of the history of feminism. Several women who had been closer to the movement (including one former leading radical feminist, whose role – and mistakes – were described at length in the book) argued that these things *had* happened, that they were in fact an important part of the history of the women's movement, and that if we wanted to build another movement we had better look carefully at these problems, because similar things could happen again. The point I am trying to make is not that Echols's, or Carson's, accounts are unchallengeable – but that challenging them by suggesting that it is racist or sexist to criticize SNCC or radical feminism (or that such criticism should be avoided because it makes the movement vulnerable to its enemies) only makes it more difficult to think about these histories.

The two stories about discussions of Echols's book are stories about fears of sexism getting in the way of discussions among feminists. Self-intimidation also gets in the way of people talking with one another across divisions of race, gender, or ethnicity. For example, a coalition of student groups, calling itself the Student Antiwar Coalition, played a major role in Spring 1991's quite impressive antiwar mobilization on the Santa Cruz campus. One of the member groups was a progressive Jewish student organization. Several weeks into the war members of this organization became uncertain that they could continue to oppose the war; their representatives reported this to the coalition. The coalition, instead of regretting the departure of this group, decided to abandon the name "antiwar coalition" and entered a period of crisis about its own identity and role. Evidently the fear of being seen as anti-Semitic overrode the desire to maintain clear opposition to the war. In the faculty antiwar organization, the issue that we never managed to discuss was the Israel-Palestine question—out of the fear that there might be conflict, and I think out of a deeper fear that positions might be expressed that might be interpreted as anti-Semitic.

The problem is not just self-censorship. There are also overt attempts to define certain areas as off-limits for discussion. Many people in the organized Jewish community have habitually equated criticisms of Israel with anti-Semitism and have been ready to call any Jewish person who consistently makes such criticisms a self-hating Jew. This has been a problem not only for Jews who are critical of Israel and do not want to be written out of the Jewish community, but for the peace movement as a whole. The mainstream peace organizations were caught off guard by the Gulf War—partly because these organizations have tended to avoid addressing the question of the Middle East, out of a fear of being called anti-Semitic for taking stands at variance with those of the mainstream Jewish organizations. Sensitivity to anti-Semitism is legitimate: anti-Semitism is very much alive, and the war was an occasion for widespread expressions of it. But it does not help the fight against anti-Semitism when charges of it are used to silence one side of a legitimate debate. And even when what is at stake is actual bias, silencing discussion doesn't help. To use the example of anti-Semitism again: there seems to have been a lot more progress toward its elimination in West Germany, where it has been an open topic of discussion, than in Eastern Europe, where it was driven underground by being made a crime – and simply continued to fester.

This is certainly not the first time that the fear of saying something wrong has stifled discussion in progressive movements. In the Communist party we called it "correct lineism." Unfortunately the tendency to use ideology as a weapon against others in the same movement has not been limited to Communists or other Marxist-Leninists. Virtually every sector of the radical movement was overcome by this dynamic in the late sixties. In the antiwar movement it was accepted practice for leading activists (mostly men) to browbeat other activists (often women) by wielding what they regarded as a superior political line. Nor was this behavior limited to white men. The same dynamic was replicated within the women's movement and the black movement, as well as in the interactions among all these movements.

Political correctness – or, more generally, the tendency to use ideology as a bludgeon – is always a danger for a social movement. It can appear in movements with very different aims and ideologies; it can appear in movements that are strong as well as those that are weak. It takes different forms under different circumstances. The "correct lineism" of the Marxist tradition involved a humorless, singleminded focus on results; it meant putting a particular objective ahead of everything, including democratic discussion that might go against pursuing this objective. Today's political correctness comes out of a movement, or a political atmosphere, that is dominated by identity politics. It is more oriented toward moral than strategic thinking; it often seems more concerned with what language is used than with what changes are made in the social structure. The danger is not so much regimentation as preachiness, a search for moral self-justification, the assigning of moral status in terms of exclusion or subordination, and the use of moral judgments as clubs against ourselves and others.

Perhaps today's political correctness bears some relation to the peculiar situation in which progressives find ourselves in the eighties and nineties: we have considerable cultural influence, at least in some arenas (notably the university and intellectual circles), but virtually no political clout. This state of affairs can lead to frustration, cynicism about the possibility of political effectiveness, and a temptation to focus on berating one another rather than finding grounds for unity.

The appeal of identity politics is no doubt partly due to the fact that the identities that have become the main basis for radical discourse are often uncertain or fragile—especially for young people. Enormous numbers of people of color in the United States are racially mixed: one parent may be white, or the two parents may come from different groups of color. This is probably more the case for younger generations than older ones, and particularly true among the young people of color of relatively privileged class backgrounds; thus it is an issue for many students of color. Lesbian and gay identities can also be fragile: a student who defines him- or herself as homosexual today may adopt a different definition tomorrow. Adopting a political identity as a Jew is—for many Jews—problematic, given the political positions that it connotes, and also given the long history of Jewish involvement in a more broadly defined Left. Self-definition as a woman is stable, but its meaning may be very different for different women, and for the same woman at different point in her life. In any event the women's movement does not have the same vitality on today's campuses as movements of gays, lesbians, and people of color.

A politics based on identity encounters not only the problem of the fragility of particular categories of identity, but the fact that everyone occupies various categories at once. One may be female but white, or black but male; virtually everyone is vulnerable to some charge of privilege. The language of political correctness is saturated in guilt—from which no one is immune. In a world of shifting identities, emphasizing one's difference from others can give organizations, and people, a sense of security. But it can also get in the way of efforts to find common ground for action. I am not arguing that we should soften our opposition to racist, sexist, and homophobic language. I am arguing that a politics that is organized around defending identities based on race, gender, or sexuality forces people's experience into categories that are too narrow and also makes it difficult for us to speak to one another across the boundaries of these identities—let alone create the coalitions needed to build a movement for progressive change.

Gay and Lesbian Studies
for Everyone

■ ■ ■

MARTIN DUBERMAN

■ ■ ■

L ESBIAN AND GAY studies, almost unimaginable a decade
ago, has explosively emerged in the past few years as a field
of scholarly inquiry. The development is international in scope,
with recent congresses convened in Canada, the Netherlands,
and the United States, and with the publication of academic journals in many countries, including Italy, West Germany, and England.

The two most conspicuous centers for lesbian and gay studies
are the United States and the Netherlands. At the Universities of
Utrecht and Amsterdam full programs have come into existence,
offering courses and research grants and employing full-time faculty. In the United States, an undergraduate major in gay and lesbian studies is offered at the College of San Francisco; a variety of
courses are being given at (among others) the Massachusetts Institute of Technology, Yale, and Duke; and a research center, designed along the lines of the Kinsey Institute, is about to open its
doors at the Graduate Center of the City University of New York.

Why this extraordinary flurry of activity? And can it be justified as a source of information and enlightenment for *non*-gays?

The answer to the first question comes in two parts. The first is
in the political arena: the advent of an organized lesbian and gay
political movement in the late sixties. Not only did that movement
create a more tolerant climate, it also challenged certain ortho-

doxies, particularly psychological theories that had long linked homosexuality and pathology, that for decades had hindered new ways of thinking about sexuality in general.

The second development that helped to foster gay studies was in the world of history itself and the recent ascent of social history. The emphasis in social history on the lives of so-called ordinary people, on the private world of intimacy, and on the structures of everyday life are precisely the concerns that characterize the work of gay and lesbian historians, legitimizing that work as a logical extension of the concerns of all the new social historians. This is not to say, of course, that the academy has swung in the other direction, embracing gay and lesbian studies with open arms. To the contrary, many traditional academics still regard the study of homosexuality as at best a marginal enterprise, at worst an embarrassing, distasteful development spawned by political polemics rather than in any organic scholarly necessity.

But gay and lesbian studies have already demonstrated that they are of significance not just to gay people, but to everyone. The scholarly work generated to date has included pioneering information about a number of matters of overriding importance to us all: The history of sex roles; the relationship of gender to sexuality; the processes of forming both personal and community identities; the workings of ethnic and interest group politics; the ways in which minority styles and values come to influence mainstream culture.

Above all, perhaps, reclaimed gay and lesbian experience has shown that it has much to say to everyone about the plasticity, resourcefulness, and diversity of human nature in general. The history of gay people in the Western world is not, after all, merely the story of repression. It is also the story of resistance and survival. And because of that, it provides unique information about how human beings who are "different," and who insist on exploring and expressing that differentness, pursue their lives in the face of adversity and oppression.

It is my belief that we are all different in our own—not necessarily sexual — ways, and that we are *all* more uniquely packaged than most of us care to admit. The courage to be different is at the heart of the true history of gay people in the West. And as such it can provide insight and courage to anyone striving to discover his or her special nature — and to insist it be respected.

Gay and lesbian studies, like all multicultural enterprises, is about differentness and connection. It is about how we are not carbon copies of one another, but are all human. And we become most fully human when we move toward, rather than away, from one another.

Stereotypes and Sensibilities

■ ■ ■

SHAWN WONG

■ ■ ■

RICHARD RODRIGUEZ, in *Hunger of Memory*, described
the beginning of his public school education as the beginning of a "betrayal" of his family. The cultural boundaries of his
family's life were lost to the start of his American public school
education. In his essay "An American Writer," Rodriguez writes,
"America is the country where one stops being German, stops
being Chinese. Where grandmothers stand at windows, mistrust-
ing, deploring, partaking."

I attended the second grade in Taiwan. Given my last name,
this is perhaps not a startling revelation. What was startling about
this experience was that I was born and raised in Berkeley, California. I spoke no Chinese. In Taiwan I was enrolled in an all-
American, predominantly white U.S. Navy school. On the school
bus that first day the children chanted, "No Chinese allowed!" I
thought they were referring to my mother.

My elementary school education began in the fifties in Berkeley and was scattered all over the Pacific Islands and California—
eleven schools from kindergarten through high school. My memories are predominantly of being the "new kid," the outsider, of
having to answer the question "What are you?" I never thought I
was much different from my classmates until that experience in
Taiwan. The consistently monocultural education offered in the
eleven public schools I attended spoke to our common backgrounds, made us a homogeneous school population, but did not
inform us about the kid sitting next to us, let alone a global
neighbor.

The irony today is that some school districts in California—for example, schools in Santa Clara County—predict not only that they will be predominantly "minority," but also that, specifically, they may be more than 50 percent Asian by 1994. The change in curriculum to meet the needs of our new American identity must begin not at the public school level but in the institutions of higher education that train our teachers. While the push in colleges and universities for American ethnic studies requirements is a minuscule step toward preparing students for a changing America, those steps are often met with great resistance.

Those who oppose transformation of the curriculum say they fear the "classics" of Western European culture or the traditional liberal arts education will be relegated to second place in academia's priorities. They fear the classical American university education is being threatened, in the name of cultural diversity, by a new educational activism that will take over the curriculum instead of buildings. The problem is that the monoculturalists and academic traditionalists want us to believe that the movement towards multiculturalism is a kind of reverse racism when, in fact, it is the monoculturalists who do not apprehend reality: the language and the images of our society have already changed.

America is already a multiracial and multicultural society, not, as some would have us believe, merely approaching this state. We are there. The nation has changed in numbers and in language. And what the naysayers fail to note is that many of the moves to change college and university curricula are student-initiated. Students know they will be unable to compete in twenty-first-century America with a monocultural, monolingual education.

Much of the scholarship surrounding Asian American history and culture is infested with stereotypes, both positive and negative, from the "model minority" myth to the image of the shrewd and ruthless gang member. To say that the economic shift to Asia doesn't affect the image of Asians in America is to ignore the rise in hate crimes against Asians in America. The racial fear of hordes of Asians immigrating to America in the nineteenth century has been replaced today with the fear of a horde of Toyotas contributing to the trade deficit. In the introduction to *Aiiieeeee! An Anthology of Asian American Writers* (1974), which I coedited with Frank Chin, Jeffrey Chan, and Lawson Inada, we say: "Before we can talk about our literature, we have to explain the sensibility. Before we can explain our sensibility we have to outline our histories. Before we can outline our history, we have to dispel the stereotypes."

In our sequel, *The Big Aiiieeeee! The History of Chinese America and Japanese America in Literature* (1991), we note that much of our history was erased by ourselves in our desire to assimilate, to embrace the standard of the monocultural education that told us that "all immigrant racial and cultural groups became the object of ridicule in modern, raceless industrial society. They were foreign, alien, incompatible with modern rhythms, energies, thought processes. They were warnings to the modern individual of what to avoid. To be foreign was to be stupid, backward, sexually unattractive, impotent in modern society."

Remembering the Bad
Old Days

■ ■ ■

ROGER WILKINS

■ ■ ■

WHEN PRESIDENT BUSH went to Ann Arbor to warn graduating seniors about the great PC threat, I took it as a personal insult. This year I am celebrating two anniversaries of my graduation from the University of Michigan—the thirty-fifth anniversary of my graduation from the Law School and the thirty-eighth of my graduation from the College of Literature, Science, and the Arts. Bush was littering *my* place with his political cynicism.

The president informed the graduates and their families that free speech was endangered by PC. I find that weird, since I had never even heard of PC when the 1991 academic year began. But by the time the president made his ghastly commencement speech, the idea of PC oppression was a prairie fire being driven across the nation by gales of hot air. The whole thing was brought into focus for me when I debated Dinesh D'Souza on "Face the Nation." It was bemusing to listen to the former editor of the *Dartmouth Review* posing as a champion of civility on campus. I was even more bemused when I realized that D'Souza wasn't even born when I was at Michigan, a time when narrow white male hegemony had a far tighter grip on academe.

Now, don't get me wrong here. I love the University of Michigan and I had a swell time there. But I love it warts and all, the way black soldiers and sailors who fought bravely for their segregated country in the segregated armed forces loved America.

Michigan wasn't entirely civil to blacks when I went there, and incivility and insensitivity started right at the top with the regents and went on down to the lowest instructional level. The university was a white place when I arrived as a seventeen-year-old freshman in the fall of 1949. Despite the fact that most of the black students were from Michigan and our parents were taxpayers, we were made to feel like partially welcome guests, grudgingly accepted. Nobody took to the campus radio and told racist jokes or put threatening racist notes around the campus as has been done in Ann Arbor in recent years. That behavior, designed to slam blacks back into their "place," wasn't necessary. We *were* in our place, and there was precious little we could do about it.

What place was that? Our place then can be illustrated by the fact that I remember being assigned no book by a black writer in all of the years I attended Michigan. I remember no blacks in any instructional capacity whatsoever. I do remember a white teaching fellow suggesting that elevator operator might be an occupation for which I was suited.

I do not remember the subject of Africa ever being raised seriously in a classroom, nor any course offering that touched on the contributions of slaves to the nation or the slaves' struggles and their descendants' struggles for decency. Needless to say, in my seven years at Michigan, I received no instruction of any kind that suggested that anybody black, Negro, or colored had contributed anything of value to this country.

I never found material about such subjects, and there was no adult on the campus who showed the least inclination to give me assistance in that direction. I did have a faculty adviser who was relentlessly rude to me in our one meeting during my freshman year. As I was leaving, but not yet out of earshot, I heard him — speaking to a third party — refer to me as a nigger.

The texture of campus life wasn't wonderful either. My girl friend, Eve, was not permitted to try on clothes, as the white girls were, when she shopped on State Street. When I got to Michigan, no black had ever played on the basketball team. During my early college years, blacks were not served at the campus drinking hangout, the Pretzel Bell, where it was traditional to celebrate one's twenty-first birthday with friends and a free pitcher of beer. In my seven years on the Michigan campus, I never attended one party at a white fraternity or sorority. We blacks created our own rich, segregated social lives.

The student government was decent. It did try to have discriminatory clauses removed from sorority and fraternity charters, but the regents and the administration always rebuffed those efforts. It was most important, we were admonished by higher authorities, to protect the property rights of these organizations.

Michigan wasn't a uniformly racist place, and far better than most campuses at that time. There were good white people there, both teachers and students. I still have close and wonderful white friends from those days, and a couple of white adults did nurture me in very constructive ways. Moreover, some blacks were able to gain prominence in campus life. A black had been president of the LS&A class of 1949, just before I arrived. A black all-American football player, Lowell Perry, was probably the most popular man on campus our senior year. And I was president of our class.

Nevertheless, in its policies and practices, Michigan taught one overwhelming racial lesson: blacks were peripheral to the life of the nation, and their capacities to contribute were limited at best. That was a heavy burden for our young black souls to bear, and I'm sure it did some of us permanent damage.

But the white kids were at least as severely damaged. They were learning the same lessons about the capacities and human worth of people of color. Michigan wasn't unique. That was the traditional way for whites to be trained nationwide. Some people wondered why, in the next decade, the country's "best and brightest" couldn't accurately assess the political and fighting abilities of the Vietnamese enemy. I was never puzzled because I had seen how they had been educated.

The great American struggle of the last half of the twentieth century has been to throw off the self-satisfied hegemony of narrowness and ignorance that has crippled our nation for so long. Change is rarely smooth or free of rancor. Some stridency and moral rigidity can be expected from those long denied their voices, but those excesses can soon be corrected by the ordinary processes of rational discussion and debate.

There are cynical excesses in this situation, however, that arise exactly where you would expect – in the bastions of unchallenged privilege. Though it is quite disgusting for the president to cry, "Political extremists roam the land, abusing the privileges of free speech, setting citizens against one another on the basis of their class or race," this is not surprising coming from a member of the former, exclusionary and secret Yale society, Skull and Bones. What is startling about the president's utterance is that it so aptly describes Bush's own manipulation, of Willie Horton and quotas, in the nation's political dialogue.

For all its prominence in the recent drama of racial turmoil on U.S. campuses, Michigan is a far better place now than it was when I went there in the 1950s. This is largely attributable to the efforts made to diversify the student body, the faculty, and the curriculum – those efforts now labeled "PC oppression" by the snooty ol' boys who long so for the good ol' days.

Canons to the Right of Them . . .

■ ■ ■

PAULA BENNETT

■ ■ ■

> Canon building is Empire Building.
> Canon defense is national defense.
> Canon debate . . . is the clash of cultures.
> And *all* of the interests are vested.[1]

IN "UNSPEAKABLE THINGS UNSPOKEN: The Afro-American Presence in American Literature," Toni Morrison observes that

> what is astonishing in the contemporary debate [over the canon] is not the resistance to displacement of works or to the expansion of genre within it, but the virulent passion that accompanies this resistance and, more importantly, the quality of its defense weaponry.[2]

It is to the issues surrounding and generating this "virulent passion" that I wish to address this essay. Whatever its limitations, *The Heath Anthology of American Literature* is the first sustained effort on the part of America's scholarly community to come to terms with the vast wealth of our multiracial, multi-ethnic literary inheritance. As my students have repeatedly told me, working with it has proved a profoundly enriching experience,

1. Toni Morrison, "The Canon: Civil War and Reconstruction," *Michigan Quarterly Review*, vol. XXVIII, no. 1 (Winter 1989), p. 8.
2. Ibid., p. 40.

one that has brought them in touch not with the America that "ought to be" but with the America that was – and still is. They are grateful to read many of the recovered works and are sad – or, in some cases, angry – that they were not exposed to these works earlier in their lives.

But as I have also learned, for other students, working with *The Heath Anthology* is more threatening than it is enlightening, and for them, as for multiculturalism's opponents generally, this anthology is (or can be) a dangerous book. In opening up the canon to a multiplicity of voices from America's racially and ethnically excluded minorities, the anthology has challenged American identity at its core – in the dream of Adamic innocence that has historically sustained and justified it. Those who are vulnerable will see this challenge as an attack upon themselves – their values, their way of life – and they will fight it with everything in them. The virulence they bring to the canon's defense may prove, finally, the measure of the anthology's "success" in transforming our image of America's past, and present. But it also suggests that nothing is safe about the *Heath*, least of all teaching it in the charged political climate that now prevails both in the university and in the culture at large.

My students are primarily white middle-class returnees, housewives, or younger women who for one reason or another, usually economic, have gotten "off track." A good third, at least, are Roman Catholic. They are hardworking, intelligent, and interested, but their formal education has been uneven at best. When they began this course, a yearlong survey of American literature, they were familiar with the "Puritans" (always as a group), Jefferson, Emerson, Thoreau, Hawthorne, Melville, Whitman, and a few others. The first night – the class meets one evening a week for two hours and ten minutes – I gave them a choice.

"This," I said, passing out copies of the table of contents of the *Norton Anthology of American Literature*, "is what – until this year – you would have studied. I want you to compare it with the

Heath's and tell me what differences you see." A list based on categories identified by the *Heath*, but missing from the *Norton*, took
shape: native Americans, the Literature of Discovery, Women,
the Literature of the Southwest, Spanish-American, Mexican, the
Literature of Abolition. They halted. "You missed one," I said.
After a few awkward moments, "African?" a voice queried.

I then explained the concept of the canon to them: how over
time a sifting had taken place that reduced the vast body of American literature to a select group of authors, largely male, largely
white, largely middle class, who are deemed to possess exceptional literary value. There is, I observed, another way to look at
our literary inheritance, one based on inclusion, not exclusion,
and that is what the *Heath* is about. It seeks to restore the voices of
those who have been "disappeared." Did my students want to
read them, or did they want to study primarily the authors of the
mainstream? Curious and timorous at once, they voted to go with
learning what they knew nothing about.

On the whole, they have not regretted their decision. But it has
not been easy. Not for them, or for me. Early on a context evolved,
as patterns began to emerge, and this context has, effectively,
dominated everything since. It is a context that makes violence,
economic exploitation, and racism, not innocence, central to the
American experience and, therefore, to the evolution of American character and literature: Columbus (1492) urging his master
and mistress to convert the native inhabitants of America to
Christianity as quickly as possible "to gain to our holy faith multi-
tudes of people, and to Spain great riches and immense domin-
ions, with all their inhabitants; there being, without doubt, in
these countries vast quantities of gold." Cabeza de Vaca, thirty
years later, writing of the decimation "conversion" wrought: "We
passed through many territories and found them all vacant: their
inhabitants wandered fleeing among the mountains, without daring to have houses or till the earth for fear of Christians." Samuel
Purchas, early-seventeenth-century Anglican cleric, justifying
from his armchair Britain's right to colonial expansion in terms

that place the enterprise somewhere between gold-digging marriage and outright rape:

> All the rich endowments of Virginia, her Virgin-portion . . . are wages for all this worke: God in his wisdome having enriched the Savage Countries, that those riches might be attractives for Christian suters, which there may sowe spirituals and reape temporals. (p. 140)

The vision informing this literature is capped in anno Domini 1637, when the Puritan settlement under William Bradford burns alive 400 Pequot Indians in a stockaded village which the Europeans had surrounded. "It was a fearful sight to see them thus frying in the fire," Bradford records, "and the streams of blood quenching the same, and horrible was the stink and scent thereof; but the victory seemed a sweet sacrifice." A note informs readers that Bradford "thus places the Pequot War in a line of great battles waged by God's chosen people." But, for us, Bradford's "holy" war cannot be separated from the 150-year history preceding it, 150 years in which Europeans "reaped tempora[l]" what they "sowed spiritua[l]," by wiping out whole native populations in the interest of colonial expansion.

To read the Puritan account apart from this history is in some sense not to read it at all. Conversely, however, to read it within this context is to acknowledge that our country begins here – in this record of dispossession and slaughter (as well as of "discovery") – not in the "City on the Hill," let alone in the First Continental Congress.

What happens to the passage from Bradford happens throughout. Read against the writers who have been excluded from the canon, whether native American, Spanish American, black, or, merely, female, the mainstream authors become "politicized" whether one will or no. For now there is no avoiding the problems they skirt, or, even more important, ignoring the contradictions woven

into the very fabric of their lives and thought. It is the contradictions that haunt the most: Ben Franklin, decent enough to be appalled by the mindless massacre of the pathetic remnants of the
Conestoga Indians, yet callous enough to preach a doctrine of
hard work and parsimony that makes the acquisition of wealth
(not virtue) life's greatest good. Thomas Jefferson writing "All
men are created equal," yet keeping slaves. Even poor old Natty
Bumppo, having eloquently thundered against the merciless and
wasteful slaughter of pigeons, winds up killing one himself.

This contradictoriness becomes, it seems, an American way of
being, permeating women's lives and works (a Margaret Fuller's
as well as a Mary Chesnut's) along with men's. Eventually, in
Emerson, Thoreau, Whitman, the capacity for self-contradiction
will be openly celebrated. But by the time my students reach
these nineteenth-century defenses, they have inevitably acquired
a hollow ring and appear all too blatantly self-serving. Not sur-
prisingly, men like William Apes, a Pequot, writing in 1837, felt
baffled:

> But reader, I acknowledge that this is a confused world, and I am
> not seeking for office; but merely placing before you the black in-
> consistency that you place before me – which is ten times blacker
> than any skin that you will find in the Universe. . . . If black or red
> skins, or any other skin color is disgraceful to God, it appears that
> he has disgraced himself a great deal – for he has made fifteen
> colored people to one white, and placed them here upon this
> earth.
>
> Now let me ask you, white man, is it a disgrace for you to eat,
> drink and sleep with the image of God, or sit, or walk and talk with
> them? Or have you the folly to think that the white man, being one
> in fifteen or sixteen, are the only beloved images of God? (pp.
> 1756–57)

If Apes, an ordained minister in the Methodist Church, was
perplexed by the heritage that the dominant society bequeathed
him, so by this time were my students. Why, they wanted to

know, were authors such as Apes lost—authors from whom they felt they learned so much? "I know students I want to give these readings to," said one woman, who works in a high-school library. She was referring to Frederick Douglass, Harriet Jacobs, David Walker, and Henry Garnet, as well as Apes, for all these writers were "new" to her and all had moved her—and most of the other students—profoundly. Even as we discussed the racial and ethnocentric biases inseparable from canonization (for what group will not "canonize" its own?), the president asked Billy Graham to the White House so that they could pray together before the United States began its counterinvasion of Kuwait. Without my inviting it, the possibility of another kind of holy war—this one in Democracy's name—had entered the classroom.

Somewhere along the way, my students had begun to bring me presents. A bulletin on the upcoming quincentennial celebration of Columbus's landing in America: some people, the bulletin warned, see this as an occasion for mourning, not for celebration; there could be protests from a variety of quarters. An article by Walter Myers, a black writer of children's books, which observed that since Great Society funding dried up, publishers' interest in literature aimed at black children had commensurately dwindled. A review of *Dances with Wolves* by Dianne Dumanoski, in the *Boston Globe* (January 14, 1991), which quoted Donald Worster, a historian at the University of Kansas:

> "We've never had good self-understanding. . . . Our national myth is an 'imperialistic one' that celebrates conquest of the land and of other people. . . . Our history has been driven by a powerful urge to acquire wealth and power, and that has had very destructive consequences at times." Confronting and acknowledging the imperialistic strand in our culture "should help us mature as a people."

The student underlined the entire quotation.

Like the presents themselves, her italics told me what I already knew. That the issues raised by the literature collected in *The Heath Anthology* could not be confined to the classroom. They were part of the fabric of American society — the American way of life. They were there from the beginning and, as America launched its latest crusade, they were with us now. Angry — and no doubt out of line — I told my students about B.T.'s, a bar in Dearborn, Michigan, where on "Rambo Wet Panty Nights" men with black plastic Uzi submachine guns squirt water at the vaginas of scantily clad go-go dancers named Vietnam, Nicaragua, and now, I supposed, Iraq.[3]

For one student, the whole thing was too much. She vehemently objected to the way the anthology "turned the class into a political arena," and she objected to my politics as well. She was, she pointed out, a "captive audience." She was furious and I lost her. But her words touched off anxieties of my own and I worried both about my teaching and about the other students. Whether or not the war had forced this turn, the anthology — its principles, its gathered insights — had become our text, and running through it like a fiber of gold (or was it pyrite?) was Jefferson's promise of equality, a promise whose betrayal spoke to the violated vision of America, to the dream that again and again was deferred, and to the constant resort to self-justification that resulted.

I could not treat the writers in this anthology as if they were "apolitical" if I tried. Indeed, to pretend they were, or that political issues did not lie at the heart of American literature itself, would be the worst — and most politically motivated — of lies. If Bradford and Jefferson are "American" literature, then so are Douglass, the Grimké sisters, and Apes. And if this is true, then the issues I was dealing with — and which so enraged that one student — were ones I could not in all fairness avoid.

"I can't help but think of the irony in a country (*my* country) that professes to be concerned about human rights in view of its

3. See Jill Dolan, "Desire Cloaked in a Trenchcoat," *Drama Review*, vol. XXXIII, no. 1 (Spring 1989).

history with Native Americans, blacks, women," one student wrote, speaking of the Gulf War. But by the nineteenth century we were mired in other, multiplying, ironies as well. "Man's war-fare on the trees is terrible," Lydia Huntley Sigourney declares in "Fallen Forests" (1854), a poem I brought into class. In 1849, Caroline Kirkland helplessly protests the casual rapes of Western forests and the less immediately noticeable transformation of "our fields of golden grain into 'fire water' — a branch of business in which Michigan is fast improving." Meanwhile, back in Concord, America's "first" naturalist, Thoreau, lauds the "bush-whack, the turf-cutter, the spade, and the bog-hoe, rusted with the blood of many a meadow, and begrimed with the dust of many a hard-fought field." The future, he avers, lies in the West. As our conti-nent is larger, so our "intellect" will be "on a grander scale." Predictably, my students, who, by now, have had their fill of self-contradiction, want to know why Thoreau is considered so great. Just as predictably, I want to know how he — so sensitive, pre-sumably, to language — can not hear himself.

Yet ironically, it is in the work of one of F.O. Matthiessen's five "great" writers that the course, the anthology, and the present state of America do finally come together — in Melville's "Benito Cereno." For Captain Delano, the "innocent" American — whose dangerous opacity Melville saw so clearly — has never been inno-cent. We know that now. He has been implicated in the evil around him from the beginning.

But he has always managed to project his evil onto others: the Pequots, the Africans, witches, the wilderness, the White Whale, Russia, Vietnam, Iraq. The making of the "American Adam" requires that the rest of the world bear the burden of his sin, that the enemy always be other than himself.

No wonder, then, that the defense of the canon has been ac-companied by such virulent emotion. To "open up" the canon, to include the voices of those who have been excluded, is to expose the "Adamic" myth for what it is: the impregnable shield of our

corruption, the singular vision by which we have been able to justify to ourselves the crimes we have committed in our own name.
And what will we be without it? What kind of America will we
forge from the knowledge that our idealism has not freed us (*pace*
Emerson, Thoreau, Whitman) from Old World sin? That, if anything, our dreams of innocence have led us to commit further sins
that are in some sense uniquely our own? How, in short, will we
still love ourselves? How will we praise our "famous" men?

And yet a student writes:

> It's funny that it's coming together in the "recognized" writers . . .
> but I don't think I'd be coming to the same understanding without
> the "unrecognized" writers as well. . . . [R]eading the recognized
> and un-recognized voices *together* makes up a truer reading of
> American literature – To understand the lack of cohesiveness,
> the apparent contradictions in Emerson and Thoreau[,] you need
> to understand what they were ignoring (subconsciously or uncon-
> sciously), as well as what they were protesting – To appreciate
> the clarity and certainty of Douglass you have to understand how
> rare it was, what a victory it was. To understand the richness of
> Hawthorne and Melville you have to see the underlying tensions.
> To see the confusions of Wheatley and Jacobs you need to under-
> stand the tightrope of cooperation and struggle they walked

She is right, of course. There is no way to teach one set of writers without the other, however tight a rope this forces us to walk.
For both are inextricably part of a whole, that whole, America.
But insofar as inclusion of the "unrecognized" writers forces us to
be aware that American literature is, in Hazel Carby's words,
"centrally concerned with the formation of a national subjectivity
and ideology that construct and simultaneously exclude a racial-
ized other" – an "other" on whom, in turn, we have projected our
"evil" – and whom we have chosen economically as well as spiri-
tually to exploit – the teaching of American literature will never
be safe. The men with the black plastic submachine-guns – or the
black briefcases filled with "great books" and initialed, perhaps,

NAS (if not NRA) — will always be looking for some way to get back their own. "Virulent passion" will always accompany their resistance.

Postscript: Between the time I began this essay and the time I finished it, a spate of attacks on multiculturalism has appeared in the media. These attacks, ostensibly written in a "liberal" defense of free speech and free academic inquiry, have wildly misrepresented the goals, intentions, and methods of multiculturalism, identifying it, among other things, as a movement to throw out "major" authors in favor of a unilateral presentation of, presumably, third-rate (but politically correct) writers. This is nonsense, but it is dangerous and inflammatory nonsense. And its sudden and widespread popularity suggests that the real battle over the canon has just begun.

IV

BEYOND PC

■ ■ ■

The Politics of Innocence

■ ■ ■

HARRY C. BOYTE

■ ■ ■

IN *FROM BEIRUT TO JERUSALEM*, Thomas Friedman de-
picts the terrible irony of the Middle East. Palestinians and
Jews claim and draw upon the strengths, beauty, and passion of
their cultures to assert their dignity and right to self-determina-
tion – in a political language that makes engagement with the
other completely impossible.

That pattern seems disturbingly analogous to the dilemma of
liberal education today. Fueling much of the discussion of difference is a language of protest politics, drawn from the 1960s, in
which categories of the inherited canons (not only in liberal arts
but also, increasingly, in sciences and technology and the per-
forming arts) are well and usefully subverted. The alternative to
tradition, however, often is a vocabulary of political innocence. A
stance of innocence – the proposition that a group has no responsibility for what happens within institutions, based on their radical detachment from any power to influence events – wreaks
havoc with sustainable public life.

In academic terms, the language of protest suggests the concepts of resistance cultures and subaltern meanings. In this vocabulary, groups of people are oppressed by dominant categories,
terms, and images along different lines of power operation – race,
gender, class, sexual identity, ethnicity, particular ways of knowing (paradigmatically; the detached, "objective" rationalism of
science), and so on. What these groups can do in opposition is
mount a guerrilla action that develops, sustains, and affirms al-

ternative meanings: a resistance consciousness. This critique of cultural power operations, frequently associated with postmodernism, illuminates important issues. But it also produces mystified forms of power.

The movements of the 1960s adopted and inverted Cold War demonology. The Manichaean division of "Free World" and "Iron Curtain" became the purity of the movement on the one hand and the "evil" of mainstream America on the other. Martin Luther King, Jr.'s "children of light versus the children of darkness" electrified a national audience when the struggle was against patterns of segregation that degraded the elemental human dignity of blacks. The antiwar movement successfully contrasted America's idealistic rhetoric with the brutality of the Vietnam conflict.

Through these strategies, civil rights and antiwar movements based their main power—their ability to influence events—on moral appeal (though civil rights leadership also employed shrewd coalition-building savvy). A strongly polarized language of moral politics and change was much less useful, however, around other political issues or in settings of greater complexity, where a variety of forms of power operate. In the university, for instance, power grows not only from moral argument but from control over resources, distinction in one's field, supposed "intelligence," and so forth. (An especially irksome feature of postmodernism is the way it presents critiques of power operations and "truth claims" in convoluted, arcane language clearly intended to intimidate the uninitiated!)

From the standpoint of postmodernism, politics is a morality play of exhortation and protest. Today, we see a wide array of ideological combat in this vein: "prochoice" or "prolife," for and against affirmative action, or prayer in the schools, or animal rights. Campuses reflect the pattern with wars between conservatives or academic traditionalists and those who consider themselves politically correct—"PC." Every side uses the language of innocence and victimization. People have scant experience of a "middle ground" of public life where there is no eternal struggle between saints and sinners, innocents and moral monsters, but rather a dynamic, honest, and pragmatic public bargaining process among different interests, values, traditions, and ways of looking at the world.

The corruption that emerges out of moralized politics is that hierarchies of innocence are created. In postmodernism, an epistemological "preference for the oppressed" bears curious parallel to Catholic thought, especially liberation theology. Power depends upon the denial of power. Groups have a self-interest in obscuring the power resources they possess. A friend who teaches in a liberal college has her students line up by how they see their relationship to power. They compete for the end.

The Politics of Public Relations

■ ■ ■

SARA M. EVANS

■ ■ ■

T HE LANGUAGE OF INNOCENCE and victimization
does, indeed, corrupt the efforts of groups seeking access to
greater power and visibility. The use of such language makes coalitions difficult as groups make nonnegotiable demands on one
another and guard the rhetorical terrain on which they can claim
to be the "most oppressed" and therefore, ironically, the most
powerful in many coalitions. That power, in turn, further undermines the capacity of groups and individuals to acknowledge
their own victories and accept accountability.

Yet I feel the need to make the critique a double-sided one.
This critique points out how those who advocate "diversity" too
often contribute to their own divisiveness. There are other anxieties about divisiveness, however, with which I have much less
sympathy. Diversity—whether as a code word for race or gender,
or much less often for class, ethnicity, religion, sexual preference, disability, that endless list—does promise to disrupt some
comfortable homogeneities within universities, a disruption that I
find important, exciting, and essential. There are many within
our universities who find it abhorrent. Their insistence that "diversity" requires a sacrifice of "excellence" generates a different
opposition with very different moral overtones. Such attitudes remain dominant in the centers of power within academic institutions where the "power of innocence" is primarily understood as a
problem in managing public relations.

A critique of the politics of innocence should enable us to build more effective strategies for diversifying our institutions. First, we can stop privileging such claims and therefore allow for a more vigorous debate among ourselves. Lasting alliances require negotiation (as opposed to nonnegotiable demands) in which all parties become clear about their own and one another's self-interests. Second, we will be able to deal honestly and analytically with power in its various forms. In the current climate of backlash, defensive and morally righteous claims are likely to be self-defeating. What we need is to go on the offensive in a new way.

Beyond the Myths

■ ■ ■

TROY DUSTER

■ ■ ■

HOW CAN WE MAKE diversity a constructive experience? We asked the University of California at Berkeley's
students and they told us. First they gave us the Don'ts. Don't,
they said, try to fix things by putting us through three-hour sensitivity sessions designed to raise our consciousness about gender
or racial issues or homophobia. These are too contrived and short-
lived to make much of a difference.

And don't force matters by asking different cultures to party together. Black students told us whites are too busy drinking to
want to dance up a storm. White students said Chicanos and
blacks would rather be raucous than sociable. The perfectly integrated, all-university "We Are the World" dance party is a bad
idea, all sides told us, mainly because we don't all like the same
music.

What then, did Berkeley's diversity-seekers remember as their
most positive experiences when they reflected on their four years
here? Again and again, they would describe the time when an instructor had the class break into groups and work on joint projects. Engaged in a collective enterprise, they learned about other
students' ways of thinking and problem solving, and sometimes
they found friendships forming across the ethnic divide.

A more cooperative approach to learning, then, would breathe
some fresh air into the sometimes tense ethnic atmosphere on
Berkeley's campus. And a clear explanation and endorsement of
the merits of affirmative action by the school administration,

something on paper that every student would receive, read, and perhaps debate, would counteract the tension that grows in the present silence. These are two concrete recommendations our report makes.

But Berkeley is not a sealed laboratory, and students don't arrive here as tabulae rasae. They bring their own experiences and expectations; some are angry about injustices they've felt firsthand, while some are blithely unaware of their implications.

What our hundreds of interviews showed is that there is a sharp difference between the ways black and white students feel about racial politics; Asians and Chicanos fall somewhere in between. White students tend to arrive with an almost naive goodwill, as if they are saying, "I think I'll just go and have some diversity," while music from *Peter and the Wolf* plays in the background. They expect to experience the "other" without conflict, without tension, without anything resembling bitterness or hostility. Meanwhile, many blacks arrive after being told in high school that Berkeley is a tough place, an alien environment, and that in order to survive, they should stick with other black people.

Imagine then what happens in the first few weeks of the first semester. White students looking for diversity run into black students already sure that race is political, so pick your friends carefully. White students seeking easy access to a black group can quickly find their hands slapped. They might say something offensive without knowing it and get called "racist," a word they use to mean prejudging a person because he or she is black. *Why do you call me racist? Hey, I'm willing to talk to you like an ordinary person.*

But when black students use the term, they tend to aim it at a person they see participating in a larger institution that works against black people. *If you're not in favor of affirmative action, that means you're racist.*

The white student retorts: *I'm willing to have dinner with you, talk with you about ideas. I'm not prejudiced.* But the two are talking past each other, the white student describing a style of interaction and friendship, the black student talking about the set of views the white student appears to hold.

It is misunderstandings such as these, arising in an atmosphere of fierce competition, in a setting of remarkable ethnic and racial diversity, that lead some critics to jump gleefully to the conclusion that diversity is not working. But there is another, more hopeful interpretation. Berkeley's students are grappling with one of the most difficult situations in the world: ethnic and racial turf. They are doing this, however modestly, over relatively safe issues such as what kind of music gets played or who sits where in the lunchroom. Perhaps they will learn how to handle conflict, how to divvy up scarce resources, how to adjust, fight, retreat, compromise, and ultimately get along in a future that will no longer be dominated by a single group spouting its own values as the ideal homogenized reality for everyone else. If our students learn even a small bit of this, they will be far better prepared than students tucked safely away in anachronistic single-culture enclaves. And what they learn may make a difference not just for their personal futures, but for a world struggling with issues of nationalism, race, and ethnicity.

On the Virtues of a Loose Canon

■ ■ ■

TODD GITLIN

■ ■ ■

I UNDERSTAND THE "political correctness" controversy as the surface of a deeper fault line—a trauma in American cultural identity.

America's current identity crisis was precipitated by several events. First, the collapse of the Cold War denied the United States an opponent in the tug-of-war between capitalism and communism. When the enemy let go of the rope, the American "team"—constituted to hold the line against tyranny—was dropped on its collective ass. We are now on the prowl for a new enemy, something or someone to mobilize against: Noriega, drugs, Satan, Saddam Hussein, or the newest bogey: "political correctness"—a breed of left-wing academic intolerance and exclusion that ends up shackling not only free speech but free-flowing intellectual inquiry—a perversion of a sensible multicultural program of tolerance and inclusion.

Though political correctness is rightly condemned for its flights of excess, opponents often fail to separate multiculturalism from the PC version of tribalism. Indeed, some of the Right's intolerance is aimed not at the message but at the messengers: immigrants of color—mostly Asian and Hispanic—whose numbers have greatly increased on campuses since the sixties. These groups, along with African Americans and women, now want access—not just to the corridors of the academy but to its curriculum.

Let's face it: some of the controversy over the canon and the new multiculturalism has to do with the fact that the complexion of the United States – on its campuses and in the country as a whole – is getting darker. In 1960, 94 percent of college students were white. Today almost 20 percent are nonwhite or Hispanic and about 55 percent are women.

It is the confluence of these events – the end of the Cold War and the transformation of the "typical American" – that appears to have stirred up a particularly vocal reaction at this time to the multicultural movement within the academy. Just note the degree of alarm, the alacrity with which the media have jumped on this issue. *Newsweek*, the *Atlantic*, the *New Republic*, and *New York* jumped up with cover stories on race, multiculturalism, and the politically correct movement on college campuses. The *New York Times* has given extensive coverage to the PC trend. And George Bush, knowing a no-risk issue when he sees it, gave the commencement address to the University of Michigan at Ann Arbor on "the new intolerance" of political correctness sweeping college campuses, what he called "the boring politics of division and derision" – an ironic comment coming from the man who elevated race-baiting, through his Willie Horton commercials, to an art form.

In important ways, hysteria rules the response to multiculturalism. Academic conservatives who defend a canon, tight or loose, sometimes sound as if American universities were fully and finally canonized until the barbarians showed up to smash up the pantheon and install Alice Walker and Toni Morrison in place of the old white men. These conservatives act as if we were floating along in unadulterated canon until sixties radicals came along and muddied the waters. Moreover, the hysterics give the misleading impression that Plato and St. Augustine have been banned.

The tight canonists don't take account, either, of the fact that the canon has always been in flux, constantly shifting under our feet. Literary historian Leo Marx made the point that when he was in school it was a fight to get good, gay Walt Whitman into the canon, and to get John Greenleaf Whittier, Henry Wadsworth Longfellow, and James Russell Lowell out.

Still, without doubt there *has* been a dilution of essential modes of critical reasoning, the capacity to write, and a general knowledge of the contours of world history and thought. And this is to be deplored and resisted.

Indeed, there is a side of the academic conservatives argument I agree with. There are a shocking number of students not only in run-of-the-mill segments of higher education but in elite institutions who are amazingly uneducated in history, literature, and the fundamentals of logic, who don't know the difference between an argument and an assertion. There *is* a know-nothing mood in some quarters that refuses to understand that the ideas and practices of many a dead white male have been decisive in Western — and therefore world — history.

But the stupidification of our students cannot be blamed simply on shifts in the canon. Cultural illiteracy has crept into our educational process for a variety of reasons. In fact, America's higher illiteracy — to call it by a name Thorstein Veblen might have appreciated — is largely a function of the so-far irresistible force of popular culture as the shaper of popular discourse. By popular discourse, I mean not only the way we speak on the street but the way we speak as presidents and presidential candidates. This is a culture in which "read my lips" or "make my day" constitutes powerful and persuasive speech.

We live in a sound-bite culture, one that has taken anti-elitism as its sacred principle. In the United States, to master a vocabulary that is superior to the mediocre is to be guilty of disdain, of scorning democracy. Though conservatives will not be happy to hear about it, this leveling principle has the full force of market capitalism working for it, a force that insists that the only standard of value is a consumer sovereignty — what people will buy. Since what people will buy are slogans and feel-good pronouncements, it is not surprising that schools and universities have degraded themselves in a frantic pursuit of the lowest common denominator.

This said, we must also condemn the bitter intolerance emanating from much of the academic left — steadily more bitter with each passing Republican year as students who feel politically helpless go looking for targets of convenience. The Right exaggerates the academic left's power to enforce its prejudices, but is rightly appalled by a widespread self-righteous illiberalism. Academic freedom – the irreducible prerequisite of a democratic society – goes by the board when students at Berkeley and Michigan disrupt classes (whether of a prejudiced anthropologist or a liberal sociologist, respectively). With the long-overdue withering of Marxism, the academic left has degenerated into a loose aggregation of margins – often cannibalistic, romancing the varieties of otherness, speaking in tongues.

In this new interest-group pluralism, the shopping center of identity politics makes a fetish of the virtues of the minority, which, in the end, is not only intellectually stultifying but also politically suicidal. It creates a kind of parochialism in which one is justified in having every interest in difference and no interest in commonality. One's identification with an interest group comes to be the first and final word that opens and terminates one's intellectual curiosity. As soon as I declare I am a Jew, a black, a Hispanic, a woman, a gay, I have no more need to define my point of view.

It is curious and somewhat disturbing that this has become a position on the Left since, as Isaiah Berlin has eloquently pointed out in his essays on nationalism, adherents of these views walk head-on into the traditional nationalist trap – a trap that led participants of the German *Sturm und Drang* movement against French cultural imperialism, in the end, to fascism, brutal irrationalism, and the oppression of minorities.

But there is an interesting difference between the German *Sturm und Drang* and our own "Storm and Stress" reaction to monochromatic presentations of history and literature. The Romantics of that period were opposing a French-imposed imperialism. What imperialism is being imposed in the United States? Is it the hegemony of Enlightenment ideals of reason and equality, the values of universalism?

If America's multiculturalism means respect for actual difference, we should uphold and encourage this reality against the
white-bread, golden-arch version of Disneyland America.

On the other hand, if multiculturalism means there is nothing
but difference, then we must do everything we can to disavow it.
We cannot condone the creation by the Left of separate cultural
reservations on which to frolic. There *are* unities – to recognize,
to appreciate, deplore, or whatever, but at least to acknowledge.
There is America's strange admixture of individualism and conformity. There is the fact of American military, political, cultural, and – still – economic power on a world scale. There are
shared myths that cut across tribal lines. We may deplore the
ways in which America recognizes itself. Indeed, the Persian
Gulf War, the Academy Awards, or the Super Bowl are not high
notes in the symphony of civilization, though that is when our culture seems to collectively acknowledge itself. Nonetheless, the
United States is also a history, an organization of power and an
overarching culture. The world is interdependent and America is
not simply a sum of marginalities.

Authentic liberals have good reason to worry that the elevation
of "difference" to a first principle is undermining everyone's
capacity to see, or change, the world as a whole. And those who
believe that the idea of the Left is an idea of universal interdepen-
dence and solidarity – of liberty, equality, fraternity-and-sorority
– have reason to mourn the sectarian parochialism of the academic left. To mourn and to organize, so that the Right does not,
by default, monopolize the legacy of the Enlightenment.

We badly need a careful accounting of the intellectual, social,
and cultural nature and roots of the new illiteracies and con-
formities – as well as the academy's high-level efforts to integrate
hitherto submerged materials and populations.

It is not a contradiction to say that America has a real culture
and also to say that this culture is conflicted, fragile, constantly in
need of shoring up. The apparent contradiction is only its complexity. In fact, the identity we promote by way of giving lip ser-

vice to certain ideals about life, liberty, and the pursuit of happiness is riddled with contradiction, or at least with tension. Ours is not a relaxed or natural ideology, nor was the French Revolution's program of liberty, equality, fraternity. The point is that we can't maximize all values simultaneously.

That is why part of the multicultural program is very important. What is required in a general multicultural program, which is *not* a program for group narcissism, is an understanding of one's own vantage point but also the vantage point of others. If we don't infuse multiculturalism with a respect for the other, all we have is American-style tribalism — a perfect recipe for a home-grown Yugoslavia.

Defending the Gains

■　■　■

PATRICIA J. WILLIAMS

■　■　■

I AM ABOUT TO TURN forty years old. While I suppose
that makes me a Baby Boomer, I have always thought of myself as a Little Rocker: my earliest memories include the integration of the schools in Little Rock, Arkansas, by children just
about my age. My life's expanse has marked some of the greatest
social movements in this country's history: the civil rights movement, the peace movement, the women's movement, the struggle
for the rights of lesbians and gay men, children, the homeless,
and the variously abled. My forty years have traversed oil crises,
Motown, Vietnam, liberation from the female necessities of bra,
girdle, garters, and straightened hair, and the entire span of Justice Thurgood Marshall's remarkable career.

My age also places me (along with Clarence Thomas) among
the very first affirmative action candidates. In the fall of 1969, I
entered college as one of fifty-nine blacks; the class ahead of me
had only seven. In 1972, I entered law school in a class of only 12
percent women; the class four years later had 25 percent. While
the numbers of blacks have suffered real declines with cutbacks
in federal tuition support, very few universities in the country
have retreated to pre-1970s levels. And while women's presence
in universities remains largely ghettoized in many disciplines,
most law schools in the country have student populations that are
close to 50 percent women.

And yet forty years is still a perilously brief period in the history of social movement. If my life is representative at all of other

first-generation affirmative action Little Rockers, we are just beginning to make an impact; now is the time when our intellectual tenure and cultural power could mark or shake or shift or build upon that bedrock of consensus rather loftily called "civilization." Though women and minorities still make up a small percentage of this nation's professoriat (in law, for example, people of color account for 3 percent of the total, and all women for only 24 percent; in most other disciplines these figures are even worse), the benefits of such presence have been resounding. Women's studies and feminist theory have been profoundly stimulating. Latina and black women's literature is enjoying a popularity not seen since the Harlem Renaissance. Ethnic studies, Holocaust studies, multiculturalism, and global intercommunication could make this world a better place for all of us. As reactionary as the U.S. government is now, I have no illusions about it being worse than in the legally segregated, McCarthyistic, pre-legal-abortion 1950s.

At the same time, I am convinced we are poised at a dangerous political crossroads that could take us back much more than forty years. This threat is clear in the right-leaning direction of recent Supreme Court opinions and appointments, the battle over the Civil Rights bill, the rising rate of bias crimes everywhere, the technologizing of reproduction, and the slick commercialization of "formerly crude" hate-mongers from David Duke to Andrew Dice Clay. In academia, this trend has gotten an insidious boost in the right-wing attack on "political correctness." From the *Atlantic* to *Newsweek* to "This Week with David Brinkley," there has been a relentless assault on the views of those lumped together hyperbolically as "black activists, militant homosexuals, and radical feminists," charging them (us? could that really be me?) with "politicizing" curricula, pushing "intellectual conformity sometimes enforced by intimidation," and turning "whining" into the science of "victimology."

I think that what is going on in the attack on us liberals and Little Rockers is nothing less than *intellectual blockbusting*. I remember when I was little, in the late fifties, two or more black families moved into our neighborhood, where for fifty years my family had been the only blacks. I remember the father of my best friend, Cathy, going from house to house, warning the neighbors, like Paul Revere with Chicken Little's brain, that the property values were falling, the values were falling. The area changed overnight. Whites who had seen me born and baked me cookies at Halloween and grown up with my mother fled for their lives. ("We'd have to hold our breath all the time because colored people smell different," said Cathy with some conviction about the pending move. Cathy, who was always a little slow about these things, had difficulty with the notion of me as "colored": "No, you're not" and then, later, "Well, you're different.")

The mass movement that turned my neighborhood into an "inner city" was part of the first great backlash to the civil rights movement. I think we are now seeing the second great backlash, waged against the hard-won principles of equal opportunity (disguised as a fight about reverse discrimination and "quotas") in the workplace and in universities-as-feeders for the workplace.

On campus, the enemies of diversity are trying to make universities more like fortresses against the siege of those who are perceived to be uncivilized heathen. (Wherever 3 percent or more of us are gathered, it's a siege, I guess.) The cry has been sounded: the standards are falling, the standards are falling.

The story of my inner-city neighborhood would have been vastly different if Cathy and her family had bothered to stick around to get to know the two nice black families who moved in. Similarly, the future of U.S. universities—particularly in the hoped-for global economy—could be a fascinating one if campus communities chose to take advantage of the rich multiculturalism that this society offers. We face a quite disastrous intellectual crisis, however, if our universities persist in the culture-baiting that has brought us the English-only movement, the brazen presumption that any blacks seen on campus don't deserve to be there (in effect, the "Bensonhurstification" of the Ivy League), and the mounting levels of verbal and physical violence directed against people of color, women, Jews, Arabs, lesbians, and gays.

Given this, it is all too easy to spend a lot of time being defensive. We've all heard the silly lameness of the retorts into which these attacks box us: "I am too qualified!" "Vote for me but not because I'm a woman!" But it doesn't work. Powerful cultural stereotypes are simply not dispelled by waving your degrees in people's faces. (That's precisely ultraconservative Dinesh D'Souza's whole premise in his much-touted book, *Illiberal Education:* that an Ivy League degree just isn't worth what it used to be now that the riffraff has moved in.)

So enough. Our hardest job in these times is not to forget *why* we (the effete lefty rainbow troublemakers who plot the demise of Dead White Canon-meisters are where we are. We cannot forget the strength and comfort of our coalitions, the sacrifice that went into our fragile presence in organizations from grass-roots level to the headiest groves of academe. And we cannot forget that our biggest task in all this is coming together – not merely to overcome the sense of personal diminishment, but to fight *collectively* the persistent devaluation of our intellectual contributions. Recently, for example, I guest-lectured in the class of a constitutional law professor who was teaching disparate impact cases. As I spoke about shifting demographics and white flight, the class grew restless, the students flipping pages of newspapers and otherwise evidencing disrespect. Afterward, the two or three black students congratulated me for speaking so straightforwardly, and for using the words *black* and *white*. I later asked the professor, how is it possible to teach cases about racial discrimination without mentioning race? I just reach the neutral principles, he replied; I don't want to risk upsetting the black students. (And yet it was clear that those most upset were the white students.)

This tendency to neutralize is repeated throughout the law school curriculum: "core" classes carve off and discard some of their most important parts – like welfare and entitlement programs from tax policy, consumer protection law from commercial contract. And even though the civil rights movement was one of the most singularly transformative forces in the history of constitutional law, very little of it is taught in basic contract law classes. (When I took con law, we spent almost four months on the Commerce Clause.) Some schools – and by no means all – pick up the pieces by having such optional courses as Poverty Law, Law and Feminism, or Race and the Law. It is no wonder that the Rehnquist court can cavalierly undo what took so many lives and years to build: the process of legal education mirrors the social resistance to antidiscrimination principles. Subject matter considered to be "optional" is ultimately swept away as uneconomical "special" interests – as thoughtlessly in real life as it has been in law schools.

And the smooth bulwark of "neutral principles" is one way of avoiding the very hard work that moral judgment in any sphere requires, the constant balancing – whether we act as voters, jurors, parents, lawyers, or laypeople – of rules, precepts, principles, and context. I have always thought that developing the ability to engage in such analytical thought is the highest goal of great universities. Yet even this most traditional of educational missions is under attack. "Should [parents] be paying $20,000 a year to have their children sitting there, figuring out how they feel about what they read?" asks James Barber, founder of the neoconservative National Association of Scholars at Duke University. His question underscores the degree to which the right-wing fear of Balkanized campuses is in fact the authoritarian's worst nightmare of a world in which people actually think for themselves.

But even assuming no hostility to the incorporation of issues of race, class, and gender into the curriculum, understanding their profound sociopathology in all of our lives will take years of patient unraveling. Consider the criminal law scholar who taught a class on rape law in an undergraduate seminar of about fifteen women. The professor asked them to write essays on their experiences with date rape, which they then shared in class. While I have much to say about the pedagogical problematic of such an assignment in the first place, I will hold my tongue here, for by student account the exercise was a successful one that felt safe, moving, and empowering. The next semester, however, he took those same essays and read them aloud to the snickers of his largely male class of about 150 criminal law students. This time it was clearly an exercise in voyeurism and disempowerment. Several of the women in that class were so upset they cried or walked out. Facing complaints, the professor professed bewilderment: "Are you saying a man can never teach rape?" "I was just letting the women speak in their own voices." "This was no different from what I did last semester and no one complained."

Learning to see the differences, to understand the pernicious subtlety of what it means to live in a culture of pornography or racism—these are the issues we must be debating in universities. These are the considerations that will best humanize our pedagogy in lasting ways.

As a footnote to this vignette, I daresay it would not come as a great surprise if I mentioned that the real issue got sidetracked by a discussion of the professor's First Amendment rights to academic freedom. The First Amendment, however, has little if anything to do with the real crisis facing our campuses. I'm willing to assume that there's a constitutional right to say anything, anywhere, anytime. But this does not answer the dilemma of how to deal with the concerted propaganda of violence that is subverting any potential for creativity in higher education today.

I want to know, for example, what to do about a black female colleague who went into teaching after a distinguished career as a civil rights litigator. After one year she quit. Among the myriad horror stories she recounts (and that too many of us can recount): A student came to her and told her that there was a bullet with her name on it. At first I thought she was using some kind of awful metaphor, but it turned out that another of her students had actually taken a bullet, carved her name on the side of it, and was showing it to his classmates. (Although the dean of the law school casually promised to mention it to a psychiatrist friend, there was absolutely no institutional response of any sort to this incident.)

Predictably, the ability to mount a campaign of harassment depends on muffling the cries of resistance. In campus politics, this has come in the form of right-wing efforts to disparage the language of resistance: attacks on "sensitivity" as "mental vegetarianism"; charges of sexism, racism, and homophobia as the products of whining immaturity, and victimization as the brewed concoction of practitioners of that dark science, "victimology."

Yet the ability to be, yes, dammit, *sensitive* to one another is the essence of what distinguishes the joy of multiculturalism or willing assimilation from the oppression of groupthink and totalitarianism. When I was visiting Durham, North Carolina, during the Helms-Gantt election last year [1990], a friend of mine said she wanted me to see something. Without any explanation, she drove me over to the Chapel Hill campus of the University of North Carolina and dragged me to the center of campus. There, right in front of the student union, was a statue titled "The Student Body." It was a collection of cast bronze figures, slightly smaller than life-size. One was of an apparently white, Mr. Chips–style figure with a satchel of books on his back, pursuing his way. Another was of a young woman of ambiguous racial cast, white or maybe Asian, carrying a violin and some books and earnestly pursuing her way. A third figure was of a young white woman struggling under a load of books stretching from below her waist up to her chin. Then two white figures: a young man holding an open book with one hand; his other arm floated languidly downward, his hand coming to casual rest upon a young woman's buttocks. The young woman leaned into his embrace, her head drooped on her shoulder like a wilted gardenia. In the center of this arrangement was the figure of an obviously black young man. He was dressed in gym shorts and he balanced a basketball on one finger. The last figure was of a solemn-faced young black woman; she walked alone, a solitary book balanced on her head.

It turned out that I was about the only one in the state of North Carolina who hadn't heard about this statue. A gift from the class

198 / BEYOND PC

of 1985, it had been the topic of hot debate. Some students, particularly black and feminist students, had complained about the insensitivity of this depiction as representative of the student bod(ies). Other students said the first students were just "being sensitive" (invoked disparagingly, as though numskulledness were a virtue). At that point the sculptor, a woman, got in on the act and explained that the black male figure was in honor of the athletic prowess of black UNC grads like Michael Jordan, and that the black female figure depicted the grace of black women. The university, meanwhile, congratulated itself publicly on how fruitfully the marketplace of ideas had been stimulated.

As I stood looking at this statue in amazement, I witnessed a piece of the debate-as-education. Two white male students were arguing with a black female student.

"You need to lighten up," said one of the men.

"But . . . " said the black woman.

"Anyway, black women *are* graceful," said the other.

At the end, the black woman walked off in tears, while the white men laughed. There is a litany of questions I have heard raised about scenarios like this: Why should the university "protect" minority students against this sort of thing? Don't they have to learn to deal with it?

Let me pose an alternative set of my own: Why should universities be in the business of putting students in this sort of situation to begin with? Since when is the persistent reduction of black men and all women to their physical traits "educational" of anything? How is it that these sorts of ignorant free-for-alls are smiled upon by the same university officials who resist structuring curricula to actually teach the histories of minorities and women?

Syndicated columnist Nat Hentoff is very insistent that the solution to the campus multiculturalism struggle is to just talk about it, one-on-one, without institutional sanction or interference. But this solution makes only certain students – those who are most frequently the objects of harassment – the perpetual teachers not merely of their histories, but of their very right just to be students.

This is an immense burden, a mountainous presumption of non-inclusion that must be constantly addressed and overcome. It keeps us eternally defensive and reactive.

Nor is this issue of legitimacy merely one for students. The respect accorded any teacher is only in small — if essential — part attributable to the knowledge inside one's head. (If that were all, we would have much more respect for street-corner orators, the elderly, and the clear uncensored vision of children.) What makes me a teacher is a force lent to my words by virtue of the collective power of institutional convention. If faculty do not treat women as colleagues, then students will not treat women as members of the faculty.

An example to illustrate the dimension of this problem: A poetry reading at a school where I once taught, a casual event. A white male student in one of my seminars stood up and read a poem attributed to Rudyard Kipling, comparing the relative lustiness of white, brown, yellow, and "nigger" women. In the silence that followed his reading, I asked to go next. I read a short prose poem about my great-great-grandmother having been raped at the age of eleven by her master, my great-great-grandfather. I made no other comment.

The next day, the student went to another faculty member and complained that I seemed unduly upset by his reading; he said he was afraid that I would not be able to grade him objectively, and he would be subjected to the unfairness of my prejudice. The faculty member's response was, "I'm sure you two can work it out."

Now the one thing that this student and I could quickly agree on was that this was a deeply unsatisfactory resolution: in reducing the encounter to one-on-one, this suggestion ignored the extent to which what was going on was (for both of us) a crisis of power, a dislocation of legitimacy. This was no mere difference of individually held opinion, and it could not be resolved at that level. For the university community to act as though it could be was to abandon its function as a player in the moral debate about the propaganda of human devaluation.

The dilemma I face at this moment in the academic world is this: If I respond to or open discussion about offensive remarks from students in my classes, I am called "PC" and accused of forcing my opinions down the throats of my students – and of not teaching them the real subject matter. If I respond with no matter what degree of clear, dignified control, I become a militant black female who terrifies "moderate" students. If I follow the prevalent advice of "just ignoring it," then I am perceived as weak, humiliated, ineffectual, a doormat.

It's great to turn the other cheek in the face of fighting words; it's probably even wise to run. But it's not a great way to maintain authority in the classroom – in a society that abhors "wimps" and where "kicking ass" is a patriotic duty. In such a context, "just ignoring" verbal challenges from my law students is a good way to deliver myself into the category of the utterly powerless. If, moreover, my white or male colleagues pursue the same path (student insult, embarrassed pause, the teacher keeps on teaching as though nothing has happened), we have collectively created that peculiar institutional silence that is known as a moral vacuum.

And that, I think, would be the ultimate betrayal of forty years' worth of hard-won gains.

The Multicultural West

■　■　■

REED WAY DASENBROCK

■　■　■

WHEN WE SPEAK of a common Western culture or, more narrowly, of a common European culture, we are speaking of something that took millennia to construct and consolidate. There was no common European identity two thousand years ago, just a collection of disparate peoples and cultures ranging from the world's most powerful and sophisticated, the Roman Empire, to the rude Germanic and Celtic peoples of the North. By now, it is those rude, uncivilized people who seem to stand at the center of European culture. Joseph Conrad's brilliant frame for *Heart of Darkness* reminds his British readers of 1900 that Britain, by then the very center of European civilization, was once also a "heart of darkness," considered by its Roman conquerors to lie at the outer edges of civilization.

What created the relative coherence of European culture we see today out of this multiplicity of peoples, cultures, and traditions? Contemporary thinking usually answers, *domination* – assuming that we always go on being ourselves until someone else overpowers us. However, though force undoubtedly played a role, Europe did not take shape primarily through conquest or forcible assimilation. (The Roman conquest of Britain left a few ruins but had little lasting effect.) It was created primarily by cultural imitation, the mysterious process by which one culture responds to the influence of another. Indeed, the key moment in the creation of a European culture was not the initial sudden emergence of essential Western concepts such as democracy in Athenian Greece. It was, instead, the more gradual process by which another society – Rome – underwent Hellenization and took over Greek ideals and culture as its own. Differences remained, but cultural influence and imitation created a degree of commonality such that we can speak with some accuracy of a shared Greco-Roman or classical civilization. Virgil thus is in a sense more important in the creation of "Western" culture than Homer precisely because of his acceptance of Homer as a normative ideal. This process of imitation, repeated many times over, gives birth to the essential Western concept that culture is not autochthonous, that it comes from somewhere else: from the East, if one is a Midwesterner or Westerner; from Europe, if one is American or Russian or Australian; from the Continent, if one is British; from the Mediterranean, if one is Nordic; from Greece, if one was Roman. Culture thus is not what we do but usually what someone else does better than we do. This relation is always double-edged: the provincial side both resents and admires the sophisticated side in the relationship. But there is never any ambiguity about which is the sophisticated side: it is, simply, the side that is the object of imitation over the long term.

Now this sense of culture as something learned, something constructed, something that we share with and take from others, is in quite sharp contrast to the anthropological sense of culture as the ensemble of practices of a given community. The difference is between a normative, or prescriptive, and a descriptive concept. Culture in the normative sense is what we ought to do; for an anthropologist culture is what a given people do. The anthropological sense seems to govern the current use of the term among multiculturalists, particularly in their assumption that it is important to "preserve" the culture of minority students. African Americans should study African and African American literature to maintain their own cultural identity as African Americans, and it is partly for this reason that it is deemed important to have African Americans – not members of other groups – teaching these subjects. Yet the educational practice urged on the society as a whole by multiculturalists is deeply Virgilian. Multiculturalists urge members of the mainstream culture to learn about other cultures so that we can learn from them as well as learn about them. Diversity in the curriculum is seen as important because other cultures have traits to learn from; the project is for our students and our society to become more multicultural, not simply to be more informed about other cultures. And if we are to become more multicultural, then we must consciously become a combination of what we wish to retain from our culture and what we wish to adopt from that of others. We must become like Virgil. And it is for the same reason that this project is also resisted so strongly: those opposed to multiculturalism are just as Virgilian, insisting that we should model ourselves on the models we have long imitated, not on "alien" traditions and ways of being.

However, those on both sides who present Western culture and multiculturalism as if they were opposed options miss what I would call the fundamental multiculturalism of Western culture, the fact that it has been constructed out of a fusion of disparate and often conflicting cultural traditions. The straw man of the multicultural polemics is now the dead white European male or the Anglo; only twenty years ago the straw man of comparable polemics was the white Anglo-Saxon Protestant. Whatever happened to the WASP?

In just one generation, it would seem, the once crucial distinctions between Protestant and Catholic, between Protestant and Jew, between Anglo-Saxons and other European ethnic groups have ceased to matter: all of these groups are seen to be part of a homogeneous "Eurocentric" tradition. But these internal barriers inside the "Western tradition" in America did not go away magically or easily, any more than the internal barriers inside of Europe did. One might remind anyone glibly referring to "the European tradition" (as if it were a harmonious whole) of the long conflict from 1914 to 1945 (or really from about 1500 to 1945) concerning who was to dominate Europe; one might remind anyone glibly talking about a homogeneous Anglo culture in the United States of the intense resistance, as recently as 1960, to the election of the Irish Catholic John F. Kennedy to the presidency. If we can talk about European unity or about a certain unified "Anglo" culture in this country, it is only as a result of a long historical process of knocking down the walls that have separated the different European communities. And that process is not complete even today.

The wall that multiculturalist slogans create between *just one* Western culture and non-Western culture thus reflects a kind of amnesia. Moreover, the disparate elements out of which "Western culture" has been created are themselves often non-Western in origin. One of the loci of the recent debates has been the argument advanced in Martin Bernal's *Black Athena* and elsewhere that classical Greek culture is deeply indebted to Egyptian (and therefore to "black") culture. The debate here is really about the extent to which Egyptian culture can be said to be African. For there is no disputing the obvious debt of Hellenic culture to ancient Egyptian and Near Eastern cultures. However the details of this particular controversy sort out, the imitativeness of Western culture – its ability to learn from cultures outside the West as well as from other places inside the West – has obviously been one of its constitutive features. We might broaden T. S. Eliot's dictum and say that "immature cultures borrow, mature cultures steal."

After all, if the heritage of classical civilization is one key strand in Western culture, the second key strand would have to be Christianity. For it was really Christianity, not the classical heritage, that cemented a sense of European identity: the fundamental affirmation of European identity has come from Europeans defining themselves as Christian in opposition to cultures that were seen as heathen or pagan. Yet this is deeply paradoxical. Is Christianity a Western or European religion? Its birthplace is undoubtedly "Eastern" and non-European, and it stands in close relation to other religions seen clearly as non-Western and "other," particu-

REED WAY DASENBROCK / 205

larly Zoroastrianism and Islam, or whose status in this cultural geography is problematic, particularly Judaism. If one master concept could be said to crystallize a Western mind-set, it is probably not democracy—which so many European countries managed to do without for so long—so much as monotheism. Monotheism allowed us to justify conquest of the "pagan" and "idolatrous" countries of the non-Western world; it also, by removing the sacred from the natural world to a metaphysical realm, justifies thinking of the natural world as something to be used, transformed, and conquered. Yet monotheism is an indigenous notion nowhere in Europe. It was introduced to Europe by Christianity, but derived immediately from Judaism, and ultimately from Zoroastrianism. This helps to explain why, if classical civilization and Christianity are the two more important strands or constitutive elements of Western culture, it took an immense synthesizing labor across centuries to bring them into some sort of harmony. Dante, Spenser, and Milton—in seeking to fuse classical culture with Christianity—are thus in a sense just as multicultural as Virgil was, and if we fail to realize this immediately, we are only testifying to how successful their work of assimilation was.

Finally, the third key element in any definition of Western culture would have to be science and technology. This is crucial both for the monoculturalist praise of the West (Jacob Neusner's insistence that "we are what the rest of the world wants to be") and the multiculturalist critique, which tends to find in other cultures a saner because more respectful attitude towards nature. Yet Western science and technology (whether we think it a good or a bad thing) is no more exclusively Western than Western religion. Even if much of it comes from the Greeks, they took their astronomy from the Sumerians and Egyptians, and we only know about much of Greek science because of the Arab role in transmitting it. It is hard to imagine "Western" science without the Chinese invention of gunpowder, rockets, and printing, without the Indian and Arab contributions to mathematics, and without the key Arab discovery of how to sail upwind.

Consider, for a final example, the "Western calendar," now sometimes resisted for imposing a common "Eurocentric" grid on the world. How many elements enter into a date such as Thursday, August 15, 1991? The name of the day comes from a Norse God, the name of the month from a Roman emperor. The year comes (approximately) from the date of Christ's birth, so is Christian in inspiration, but the numerical system is Arabic (and ultimately Indian) in inspiration. Nor is this hybridization and syncretism anything uniquely Western. For many of the world's central cultures are multicultural in the sense I am describing, made up of complex mixtures of local and borrowed elements. Even when we can find someone located univocally in what seems to be a homogeneous culture, a historical perspective shows how that culture was itself formed at some earlier point out of a multicultural context. The way in which successive European cultures rewrote the Homeric epics to trace their own history back to Greece is paralleled by the successive rewriting of the Indian epics, the *Mahabharata* and the *Ramayana*, in Southeast Asia. Indian culture is a complex mixture of indigenous Hindu and imported Muslim elements, and Islam has been a profound influence on the culture of much of Africa. Our current models of culture all seem to be either/or (Eurocentric vs. Afrocentric, Western vs. non-Western, monocultural vs. multicultural), but culture itself is both/and, not either/or. Multiculturalism is simply the standard human condition.

Now, nothing I have said so far should be controversial. I have recalled some basic historical facts. Yet the facts should lead us to see the debate about multiculturalism in an unexpected light. The choice cannot be between a closed Western tradition and openness to other non-Western traditions, for the Western tradition itself has always been open – if not always prone to admit that it is – to other cultural traditions. If you changed into or out of pajamas, took a bath, brushed your teeth, or had a cup of tea or coffee this morning, each of these activities is something we have taken from Asia. If, say, William Bennett's attitudes toward other cultures had always been dominant in the West, we would still be worshipping Zeus and trying to use Roman numerals. The very spirit of the West when it encounters another cultural practice is to say, "Is there something we can use here?" Is tobacco good to smoke? Is coffee good to drink? Is chocolate good to eat? Not every borrowing has been wise, but by and large Western culture has been immeasurably enriched by its ability to adapt to and borrow from others.

If this history teaches us anything, it is that crises of multiculturalism have deep historical roots and cannot be wished away. Early medieval England was a country riven by a schism between the indigenous culture and language of the Anglo-Saxons and the imported culture and French language of the conquering Normans: what resulted was the hybrid language of English and a profoundly hybrid and syncretic culture. Multiculturalism has emerged in the United States today out of a comparable historical exigency. On the one hand, we are faced with a new wave of immigration into the United States: our country is becoming less European, less white, more Asian and more Latin American. Europe, having for decades felt smug and superior about racial problems and tensions in America, is faced with the same phenomenon and is—if anything—considerably less prepared to deal with it. On the other hand, we and every other trading nation are faced with an increasingly integrated world, above all an increasingly integrated international economy, in which we can no longer pretend to separate ourselves from other nations. Borders are now gates, not walls, through which pour problems— drugs and too many Toyotas—but also essential ingredients such as oil. Most important, across borders now pour people. And each of these tendencies is likely to become more pronounced, not less, for the foreseeable future. How do we respond to the complex interaction of cultures that shapes the contemporary world?

My answer may seem paradoxical: we need to adopt a good deal of the multiculturalist agenda precisely because it is in keeping with the best and most important aspects of Western and American culture. The great moments of our historical tradition have been moments of contact with and borrowing from other cultures: a good deal of what was important about the Middle Ages was prompted by contact with Islamic civilization: Greek exiles in Italy helped spark the Renaissance, as did the discovery of the New World; the discovery of the spiritual traditions of Asia played an important role in British and particularly American romanticism. Our historical situation is perhaps more complex than any of these, since we are now in contact with the entire world through immigration and trade, but it is nevertheless a situation these examples will help us to understand. When faced with disparate cultures in contact (which usually means conflict), the successful response has always been assimilative and syncretic, to mix and match, taking the best of each. We now need to do this with the totality of the cultures of the world. But this doesn't represent a surrender of the Western tradition as much as a reaffirmation of it.

If this is what we need to do, how can we do it responsibly? Once we see the fundamental continuity between multiculturalism today and earlier moments in our history, the polemical anti-Western thrust of much multiculturalist rhetoric seems absurdly out of place, as does that side of multiculturalism seeking to "preserve" the culture of minority students by focusing their curriculum on their own culture. It is empty posturing to pretend to choose non-Western culture over Western culture when our task is to harmonize them and choose the best of both. To see the choice as one between Eurocentrism and Afrocentrism is to deny the very possibility of multiculturalism. The Afrocentric curriculum being advocated by some black intellectuals and implemented in some school systems is both impractical and no more multicultural than the suggestions of William Bennett and George Will. Moreover, this way of framing the issues ignores the degree of acculturation already undergone by minorities in this country. Most African Americans are no more culturally African than I am culturally German.

In any case, the thought of what could happen when hundreds of thousands of not very well-informed – even if well-intentioned – schoolteachers and college professors are turned loose on the cultures of the world is enough to make anyone cringe, and certainly what passes for multiculturalism in the nation's schools is often shallow, misinformed, and intellectually shoddy. In kindergarten, my son brought home some nationally disseminated materials about Columbus Day that made an attempt (obviously influenced by multiculturalism) to show something about precontact native American culture as well as the usual stuff about the *Niña*, the *Pinta*, and the *Santa Maria*. But the worksheet identified Columbus as landing in Bermuda, not the Bahamas; when I pointed this out to his teacher, she asked me what the difference was. In 1991, in first grade, a whole section of native American culture followed, so rife with misinformation and clichés that the children wouldn't have been much worse off just playing cowboys and Indians. I would be astonished if the new Afrocentric schools conveyed a much more accurate sense of what African culture is really like. The point here is that even the best intentions are not enough, that misinformed teaching can in fact reinforce the stereotypes and prejudices it is attempting to move beyond. Moreover, given the spirit of guardianship for these cultures dominating the attempts to represent them in the curriculum, it is unlikely that anything but a sanitized, idealized portrait of these cultures could emerge, even though it is precisely such a portrait of Western culture that multiculturalism objects to.

So a responsible and responsive multiculturalism is not going to take shape overnight. We are in for a period of experimentation, and we can only hope that more complex models and pedagogies slowly emerge and replace the simplistic visions and responses of both sides in the current debate. To anyone searching in the interim for what such a multiculturalism would look like, my advice is to read contemporary non-Western literature written in English, which seems to me to be a crucial site where we can move toward a more sophisticated sense of the world's cultures. English is an international language, playing an important role inside about one fourth of the world's 160 countries, and it has therefore become an important international literary language. Important – great – writing is being done in English all over the world, on every continent today. But this body of literature has not yet played an important role in the curriculum at any level, since it doesn't seem English or American enough to make it into the English curriculum, or "different enough" to make it into those parts of the curriculum concerned with other cultures. In this context, that is precisely its virtue. The writers themselves are often attacked from both sides, precisely because they don't fit into one camp or the other, as the case of Salman Rushdie has shown most spectacularly. In fact, the discussion about "Afrocentricity" took shape first in literary criticism when critics such as Chinweizu attacked Wole Soyinka and other African writers for their "Euromodernism." Yet the bridges these writers are building, by importing European forms into non-European contexts and by introducing non-European cultural traditions into European languages, may in retrospect seem as crucial to the formation of a world culture as the Augustan imitation of Greek culture was for the formation of classical culture and the Renaissance imitation of those classical forms and of Italian culture was for the construction of European culture.

I believe the construction of a world culture – as Wyndham Lewis said more than forty years ago and V. S. Naipaul has recently reiterated – is the task that now faces us. Despite the fashionable nostalgia for pockets of difference yet unintegrated into a world community, the alternative to such a world culture is not a lively diversity of cultures as much as unending conflict among them. Will pointing this out magically transform the current debate into a less shrill one? Of course not, for there are powerful reasons why each side in this debate wants not to understand the other. On the one hand, advocates of a separatist cultural identity for minorities reserve their harshest criticism for those of their own communities like Naipaul or Richard Rodriguez who insist that a measure of assimilation is inevitable, that accommodation must be a two-way street. Ayatollah Khomeini's condemnation of Salman Rushdie is the most conspicuous exemplification of this rage: that one of "us" could be "polluted" by contact with the other side. On the other hand, a George Will or a William Bennett finds it hard to admit that the West might have something to learn from as well as something to teach the rest of the world.

My point is not just that both sides hold to blindingly narrow ideals. It is rather that neither side perceives the world in which we live. Despite all of the talk on both sides about preserving earlier cultural identities, these identities are changing quickly and inexorably. It is in this sense that—despite the apparent polarization of the debate—the two sides are really one. Together, they represent a point of view that is historically irrelevant.

Campus Communities Beyond Consensus

■ ■ ■

JOAN WALLACH SCOTT

■ ■ ■

UNIVERSITIES HAVE CHANGED dramatically since the 1960s, and much of the present controversy has roots in those changes. In 1960, 94 percent of college students were white; the figure was 96 percent for private universities. Of the remaining 6 percent, one third attended predominantly black institutions. A number of public and private universities did not admit blacks at all, and some of the most highly regarded centers of learning did not admit women. Colleges tended to be white enclaves for students and faculty: 63 percent of college students were men, 90 percent of Ph.D.s were men, and 80 percent of university faculties were men. (When I was a graduate student in this period, the Woodrow Wilson Foundation stated explicitly that no more than one fourth of their graduate fellowships would be awarded to women.) In 1991, 20 percent of all college students are nonwhite or Hispanic, and 55 percent are women (these figures are cited in Louis Menand, "Books: Illiberalisms," the *New Yorker*, May 20, 1991, pages 101–7). Women make up over a third of all graduate students and are even more highly represented as Ph.D. candidates in the humanities; they now represent 31 percent of university faculties.

The change in university populations follows in part from a general increase in college attendance during the past several decades, but is often significantly the result of changes in recruitment policies. The expansion of the university has not so much altered admission policies as added more considerations to them and made them more visible. Admission, even to the most prestigious schools, was never based on merit alone—although that is the myth being advanced now in the anti-university campaign. Rather, merit was one of many factors that included athletic skill, wealth, geographic location, and family connections to alumni, the famous, and the powerful. The special treatment that came with high social status never seems to have been seen as a compromise of university standards. (One wonders why, for example, the test scores of blacks were stolen from the admissions office at Georgetown Law School and published by disgruntled conservatives, while those children of alumni or influential politicians were not. One can only conclude that the call for a return to a meritocracy that never was is a thinly veiled manifestation of racism.)

The new populations in the universities bring with them histories of their own that have not been part of the traditional curriculum; their presence challenges many of the prevailing assumptions about what counts as knowledge and how it is produced. This is so, first because of the sheer numbers—as well as the new kinds—of students and faculty on campuses. Is critical thinking possible when masses of students are attending college, instead of only the children of elites? Is critical thinking advisable for the masses of students, or should they (as the reports of William Bennett and Lynne Cheney suggest) be given a prescribed education that they will passively receive? Can critical thinking take place in communities that are no longer elite and homogeneous?

There have also been, in the past decades, major political and philosophical developments that have changed the way we think about relationships of difference in the world. These include decolonization of the Third World and the emergence of national identities that positively value histories and cultural practices once obscured or demeaned by colonizers who equated European standards with civilization; philosophical critiques of universalism and foundationalism and of the idea of community as a consensual, homogeneous institution; and analyses of power and differences that call attention to how "we" construct ourselves in relation to "others." If, in earlier generations, minorities adjusted to college life by assimilating to prevailing standards and accepting as universal norms that had not previously been their own, now they have the means to question the very notion of universality and insist that their experiences be taken into account.

But how is this to be done? Perhaps it is better to ask the question more historically: How has it been attempted? How have universities attempted to accommodate their different and "diverse" populations? How have demands for new approaches to knowledge been received? In some ways, the overall process today has not been all that different from previous contests about knowledge: there has been pressure for change, powerful resistance to it, as well as accommodation.

But there are also differences. Contests about knowledge are now understood to be political, not only because they are contests, but because they are explicitly about the interests of groups (rather than the opinions of individuals) in the substance and form of what counts as knowledge. It is the question of group interest and power that has been introduced into the knowledge debates and so "politicized" them in new ways. Although it sometimes takes extreme and tendentious forms, I think the explicit discussion of interest is inevitable, and it is not only minority voices that are responsible for this politicization.

A crucial point, and one regularly overlooked in hysterical pronouncements about the takeover of the curriculum, is that power is unequally distributed: those demanding change must contend with disciplinary and pedagogic practices that are institutionalized, must command resources, and must claim to have truth, rigor, and objectivity on their side. The emergence of separate courses and programs of women's studies, African-American studies, Chicano studies, and the like testify to this situation: they were created in the face of the refusal of departments to include material on these groups in existing courses and in an effort to demonstrate that they were subjects worth studying. The programs and courses, in turn, taught and attended largely by members of the groups being studied, underscored the differences in perspectives and interests that existed across the curriculum.

They also gave rise to a series of observations, highly contested, but quite serious in their philosophical as well as practical implications, about the relationships between knowledge and group identity. Does one have to be of the group to care about its history? To teach its literature? Are intellectual perspectives expressions of particular social standpoints? Does understanding require firsthand experience? What are legitimate grounds for objecting to the exclusion of whole realms of experience from so-called mainstream courses in the humanities or social sciences? What gives authority to claims for inclusion? Is it possible to teach mainstream courses from a perspective different from the one traditionally taken?

There are many answers being offered to these questions, even if the sensationalist press reports only the insistence by some blacks or women that they are uniquely qualified to teach black history or women's literature. And since they are not easy questions, the discussions are necessarily full of conflict. What is least reported these days is the fact that the disciplines, too, have exclusionary notions about who is capable of teaching what. History departments regularly refuse to consider for positions in general American history, for example, scholars who write on women or African Americans (or homosexuals or other particular groups), arguing that they are not generalists, unlike those who are no less specialists but have written about national elections or politicians' lives – subjects that are taken to stand for what the whole discipline is about.

Recently, a literature department at a major university proposed to hire in a generalist slot a scholar whose work included feminist theory. The faculty's argument that feminist theory was central to their departmental mission was not accepted as plausible by the administrative oversight committee, which turned down the recommendation.

These kinds of decisions distinguish between general and particularized knowledge according to gender, racial, and ethnic criteria, but they refuse to acknowledge that these are the terms of definition. In so doing, they perpetuate the Balkanization of knowledge, creating the conditions that necessitate separatist claims on the part of excluded groups and that fuel their frustration and anger.

My point is not to justify separatism, nor is it to endorse standpoint epistemologies. Rather, I want to suggest here that separatism is a simultaneous refusal and imitation of the powerful that must be understood in the context of the university's accommodation to diversity.

The nature of the university's accommodation to diversity can be seen in the words used to describe campuses and curricula: *diversity, multiculturalism, pluralism*. All take into account the existence of different populations with different needs and interests, but none of the words register the fact that difference is not simply a state of separate being – it is a relationship. There are no differences without comparisons, and these are usually made hierarchically in reference to something that has been established as a norm. So being black or female or gay isn't simply inhabiting a sociological category or taking on an identity that can be easily shed or disregarded. It is, instead, carrying a mark of difference (from some other group or groups) that has consequences for how you are perceived, treated, and understood in the world.

An example of how this works comes from a comment made by a white middle-class student who lived in a predominantly Latino dormitory at Stanford:

> "Sometimes I'd get confused," she said, because she never knew when a simple comment she made would offend someone else. She finally appreciated the difference between herself and the Hispanic students when one of them asked her what it felt like to be an Anglo. "I'd never heard anyone use the word Anglo for me before . . . where I came from, no one was Anglo; everyone was just Irish Catholic. But after being [here] a while, I realized that an Anglo can be an Anglo only if there's someone who's not." (Anthony DePalma, "Campus Ethnic Diversion Brings Separate Worlds," the *New York Times*, May 18, 1991, page 7)

A pluralism or multiculturalism failing to recognize that difference is a relationship — *and* that it is a structured relationship that cannot be undone simply by individual fiat or by denial of asymmetries of power — encourages separatism. Indeed, it provides the conceptual basis for it in an essentialism that denies the historical basis for difference. Each group claims a fixed, transcendant identity and argues for its unique ability to present and interpret itself. It then establishes its own canon, its own history, thereby denying the relational nature of difference and the interconnectedness — however asymmetrical and oppressive — of different groups.

S. P. Mohanty, taking up an argument made by Cornel West against a notion of separate canons, of new canons entirely replacing old, puts it this way:

> How do we negotiate between my history and yours? How would it be possible for us to recover our commonality, not the ambiguous imperial-humanist myth of our shared human attributes, which are supposed to distinguish us from animals, but, more significantly, the imbrication of our various pasts and presents, the ineluctable relationships of shared and contested meanings, values and material resources? It is necessary to assert our dense particularities, our lived and imagined differences; but could we afford to leave untheorized the question of how our differences are intertwined and, indeed, hierarchically organized? Could we, in other words, afford to have *entirely* different histories to see ourselves as living — and having lived — in entirely heterogeneous and discrete spaces? (S. P. Mohanty, "Us and Them: On the Philosophical Bases of Political Criticism," *Yale Journal of Criticism*, II, page 13)

His answer is obviously no. Instead, he calls for an alternative to pluralism that would make difference and conflict the center of a history "we" all share, "a history whose very terms and definitions are now being openly contested and formulated" (S. P. Mohanty, page 5).

University populations began to change in the 1960s and '70s, a period in which concerns for social justice were widespread, and plans were implemented to increase the possibilities for equality. Affirmative action was based on the notion that certain classes of individuals had historically been treated differently from others – not on the basis of merit or ability, but because they were perceived to be members of groups with undesirable traits and characteristics. Affirmative action took into account these historic prejudices and attempted to reverse some of their most pernicious effects – not by reversing discrimination, but by extending to blacks and women access that had historically been reserved for whites or men *as groups*.

The conceptualization of the problem in terms of groups was difficult in a society with deep individualistic strains, but not insurmountable – in part, because there are also deep egalitarian impulses that could be appealed to. In the 1980s and '90s, the ideological pendulum has swung back to individualism. The courts are reversing affirmative action decisions, the president vetoes civil rights legislation, and the history of discrimination as evident in statistics or group experience is being denied. All this is being done in the name of justice for individuals, who are conceived to be entirely equal units, living in a cultural and historical vacuum.

The logic of individualism has structured the approach to multiculturalism within the university – on many sides of the question. The call for tolerance of difference is framed in terms of respect for individual characteristics and attitudes; group differences are conceived categorically and not relationally, as distinct entities rather than interconnected structures or systems. Administrators have hired psychological consulting firms to hold diversity workshops teaching that conflict resolution is a negotiation between dissatisfied individuals. Disciplinary codes that punish "hate-speech" justify prohibitions in terms of the protection of individuals from abuse by other individuals, not in terms of the protection of members of historically mistreated groups from discrimination. The language of protection, moreover, is conceptualized in terms of victimization; the way to make a claim or to justify one's protest against perceived mistreatment is to take on the mantle of the victim. And everyone, whether an insulated minority or the perpetrator of the insult who feels he is being unjustly accused, becomes an equal victim before the law. Here we have not only an extreme form of individualizing, but a conception of individuals without agency.

There is nothing wrong, on the face of it, with teaching individuals about how to behave decently in relation to others and about how to empathize with one another's pain. The problem is that difficult analyses of how history and social standing, privilege and subordination are involved in personal behavior entirely drop out. Chandra Mohanty puts it this way:

> There has been an erosion of the politics of collectivity through the reformulation of race and difference in individualistic terms. The 1960s and '70s slogan, "the personal is political," has been re-crafted in the 1980s as "the political is personal." In other words, all politics is collapsed into the personal, and questions of individual behaviors, attitudes, and lifestyles stand in for political analysis of the social. Individual political struggles are seen as the only relevant and legitimate form of political struggle. (Chandra Talpade Mohanty, "On Race and Voice: Challenges for Liberal Education in the 1990s," *Cultural Critique*, No. 14, page 204)

Paradoxically, individuals then generalize their perceptions and claim to speak for a whole group. This individualizing, personalizing conception has also been behind some of the identity politics of minorities — indeed, it gave rise to a moralizing dogmatism that was dubbed, initially by its internal critics, "political correctness."

It is particularly in the notion of "experience" that one sees this operating. In much current usage of "experience," references to structure and history are implied but not made explicit; instead, personal testimony of oppression replaces analysis and explanation and comes to stand for the experience of the group. The fact of belonging to an identity group is taken as authority enough for one's speech; the direct experience of a group or culture – that is, membership in it – becomes the only test of true knowledge.

The exclusionary implications of this are twofold: all those not of the group are denied even intellectual access to it, and those within the group whose experiences or interpretations do not conform to the established terms of identity must either suppress their views or drop out. An appeal to "experience" of this kind forecloses discussion and criticism and turns politics into a policing operation: the borders of identity are patrolled for signs of disapproval or disagreement; the test of hostility or support for a group becomes less one's political actions and relationships of power than one's words.

I do not want to suggest that language has no bearing on relationships of power – far from it. Instead, I want to warn against the reduction of language to words; the reduction of "experience" to an idea of unmediated, direct access to truth; and the reduction of politics to individual interactions.

Furthermore, I do think that different groups have different experiences and that they offer new perspectives on knowledge that have been neglected and must be included. It is true that whiteness and femaleness set conditions of possibility and an interpretive frame for my life that they don't for a black woman or any man. But if – as S. P. Mohanty has suggested – our histories are entwined with one another, then no group is without connection or relation to any other, even if these are hierarchical, conflicted, and contradictory relationships. Groups are not isolated, separate entities, nor are individuals. I don't believe that my subjectivity sets complete limits on my ability to think about things and people other than myself, in part because who and what I am has something to do with how I am differentiated from them.

That kind of thinking about others is hard – I sometimes must be pressured to do it – and the terms of encounter with others who challenge the way I am used to thinking are not always pleasant and calm. But the encounters are at least possible when the issues are framed as issues of cognition and not of personality, when analysis and interpretation are the medium of exchange, when ideas are what is traded (however heightened the rhetorical expressions of them), and, above all, when the encounters are understood to be taking place not between discrete individuals or atomized groups, but between people who share a history, however contradictory it is.

Is it possible for universities to be centers of intellectual conflict when there are differences that cannot be resolved? I think so, but only if diversity is not conceived in individualistic terms, and if our notions of community are redefined.

If universities are to adapt to the new conditions of diversity, the notion of community according to which they operate must change. Some of the extraordinary tensions evident on campuses these days stem from attempts to impose universalist ideas of community that stress consensus and shared values on a situation in which differences seem fundamental and irreducible. The universalist idea assumes that some common denominator of interest allows "us" to articulate our common concerns and regulate our disagreements; those who do not accept the consensus are necessarily outside the community.

This is the idea that, in the name of a common culture, is invoked by those who defend the superiority of Shakespeare to, say, Toni Morrison (as if anyone was insisting that contemporary literature entirely replace "the classics"); it is the idea that underlies some disciplinary codes as well as some of the most extreme demands for political correctness. This vision of consensus ultimately requires—indeed, imposes—homogeneity not of persons, but of point of view. It rests on a set of exclusions of "others."

Something else is needed in these days of diversity and difference, and not only for the university. But the university is the best place from which to search for a different understanding of what a community might be. First of all, universities can be seen to already exemplify an alternative. They are, after all, places where separate and contingent, contradictory and heterogeneous spheres of thought have long coexisted; the grounds for that coexistence are mutual respect for difference and an aversion to orthodoxy. (Universities aren't immune from outside influences, but they process them in their own ways.) This doesn't mean there aren't continuing battles for resources, influence, and predominance; indeed, these kinds of politics are the way differences are negotiated. It does mean that there is ultimately no resolution, no final triumph for any particular brand of thought or knowledge.

Second, within the universities, the humanities in particular offer the possibility of thinking about diversity and community in new ways. There is one approach within the humanities, to be sure, that would reify a particular canon as the defining mark of our common humanity. But there is another, more complicated approach, equally available in the very fact that humanities is "humanity in the plural." Jonathan Culler puts it this way:

A particular virtue of literature, of history, of anthropology is instruction in otherness: vivid, compelling evidence of differences in cultures, mores, assumptions, values. At their best, these subjects make otherness palpable and make it comprehensible without reducing it to an inferior version of the same, as a universalizing humanism threatens to do. ("Excerpts from the Symposium on 'The Humanities and the Public Interest,'" *Yale Journal of Criticism*, I, page 187)

Add to this the fact that interpretation is the name of the game in the humanities, that meanings are always contested, reworked, revoked, and redefined, and there is at least a basis for thinking about communities in which consensus cannot prevail. Thought in these terms, the humanities become a starting point for discussion of the reconceptualization of community in the age of diversity.

I do not have a blueprint for that idea of community, but I think

there are points it must address. Here is a partial list:
- Differences are often irreducible and must be accepted as such.
- Differences are relational, and involve hierarchy and differentials of power that are constantly contested.
- Conflict and contest are inherent in communities of difference. There must be ground rules for coexistence that do not presume the resolution of conflict and the discovery of consensus.
- Communities cannot be based on conformity, but on an acceptance and acknowledgment of difference.

Christopher Fynsk, following Jean-Luc Nancy, suggests that the French word *partage* inform our notion of community (Christopher Fynsk, "Community and the Limits of Theory," unpublished paper, 1991). *Partage* means both to divide and to share: this double and contradictory meaning insists on what Fynsk calls "openings to the other" as a condition of existence. In contrast, conformity that rules out the other, substituting one set of beliefs for another, brings us the regime of yellow ribbons and American flags as the test of patriotism. It leads students to condemn dissent, as one student did at Princeton last fall [1991], as treasonous and un-American.

Partage is a more difficult concept than consensus, but a better one, I submit. It accepts difference as a condition of our lives and suggests ways we might well live with it. It lets us accommodate one another as we strive on a large scale for what is already possible in the classroom, at least in classrooms such as the one described by Elsa Barkley Brown. For her, teaching African-American women's history is not, she says,

> merely an intellectual process. It is not merely a question of whether or not we have learned to analyze in particular kinds of ways, or whether people are able to intellectualize about a variety of experiences. It is also about coming to believe in the possibility of a variety of experiences, a variety of ways of understanding the

world, a variety of frameworks of operation, without imposing consciously or unconsciously a notion of the norm. (Elsa Barkley Brown, "African-American Women's Quilting: A Framework for Conceptualizing and Teaching African-American Women's History," *Signs*, Summer 1989, page 921)

Can we achieve this kind of opening to difference in our teaching? Can universities become the place where communities of difference — irreducible and unreconcilable difference — are conceptualized and exemplified? This is the challenge we all face in the next years. It is a challenge that must be carried on, even in the face of outrageous, threatening, and punitive attacks. It is a challenge that requires the kind of critical intellectual work universities are supposed to encourage. Such critical work is, after all, the university's raison d'être and its highest form of achievement.

V

MOSAIC

■ ■ ■

GEORGE BUSH

■ ■ ■

I R O N I C A L L Y, on the 200th anniversary of our Bill of Rights, we find free speech under assault throughout the United States, including on some college campuses. The notion of political correctness has ignited controversy across the land. And although the movement arises from the laudable desire to sweep away the debris of racism and sexism and hatred, it replaces old prejudice with new ones. It declares certain topics off-limits, certain expression off-limits, even certain gestures off-limits.

What began as a crusade for civility has soured into a cause of conflict and even censorship. Disputants treat sheer force – getting their foes punished or expelled, for instance – as a substitute for the power of ideas.

Throughout history, attempts to micromanage casual conversation have only incited distrust. They have invited people to look for an insult in every word, gesture, action. And in their own Orwellian way, crusades that demand correct behavior crush diversity in the name of diversity.

We all should be alarmed at the rise of intolerance in our land and by the growing tendency to use intimidation rather than reason in settling disputes. Neighbors who disagree no longer settle matters over a cup of coffee. They hire lawyers, and they go to court. And political extremists roam the land, abusing the privilege of free speech, setting citizens against one another on the basis of their class or race.

But, you see, such bullying is outrageous. It's not worthy of a great nation grounded in the values of tolerance and respect. So, let us fight back against the boring politics of division and derision. Let's trust our friends and colleagues to respond to reason. As Americans we must use our persuasive powers to conquer bigotry once and for all. And I remind myself a lot of this: We must conquer the temptation to assign bad motives to people who disagree with us.

If we hope to make full use of the optimism I discussed earlier, men and women must feel free to speak their hearts and minds. We must build a society in which people can join in common cause without having to surrender their identities.

You can lead the way. Share your thoughts and your experiences and your hopes and your frustrations. Defend others' rights to speak. And if harmony be our goal, let's pursue harmony, not inquisition.   — *University of Michigan, May 4, 1991*

■ ■ ■

DIANE RAVITCH

■ ■ ■

THE PLURALIST APPROACH to multiculturalism promotes a broader interpretation of the common American culture and seeks due recognition for the ways that the nation's many racial, ethnic, and cultural groups have transformed the national culture. The pluralists say, in effect, "American culture belongs to us, all of us; the U.S. is us, and we remake it in every generation." But particularists have no interest in extending or revising American culture; indeed, they deny that a common culture exists. Particularists reject any accommodation among groups, any interactions that blur the distinct lines between them. The brand of history that they espouse is one in which everyone is either a descendant of victims or oppressors. By doing so, ancient hatreds are fanned and re-created in each new generation. Particularism has its intellectual roots in the ideology of ethnic separatism and in the black nationalist movement. In the particularist analysis, the nation has five cultures: African American, Asian American, European American, Latino/Hispanic, and native American. The huge cultural, historical, religious, and linguistic differences within these categories are ignored, as is the considerable intermarriage among these groups, as are the linkages (like gender, class, sexual orientation, and religion) that cut across these five groups. No serious scholar would claim that all Europeans and white Americans are part of the same culture, or that all Asians are part of the same culture, or that all people of African descent are of the same culture. Any categorization this broad is essentially meaningless and useless.

■ ■ ■

MOLEFI KETE ASANTE

■ ■ ■

THERE IS NO common American culture, as is claimed by the defenders of the status quo. There is a hegemonic culture to be sure, pushed as if it were a common culture. Perhaps Diane Ravitch is confusing concepts here. There is a common American *society*, which is quite different from a common American culture. Certain cultural characteristics are shared by those within the society but the meaning of *multicultural* is "many cultures." To believe in multicultural education is to assume that there are many cultures. The reason Ravitch finds confusion is because the only way she can reconcile the "many cultures" is to insist on many "little" cultures under the hegemony of the "big" white culture. Thus, what she means by multiculturalism is precisely what I criticized in *The Afrocentric Idea*, the acceptance of other cultures within a Eurocentric framework.

In the end, the neat separation of pluralist multiculturalists and particularistic multiculturalists breaks down because it is a false, straw separation developed primarily for the sake of argument and not for clarity. The real division on the question of multiculturalism is between those who truly seek to maintain a Eurocentric hegemony over the curriculum and those who truly believe in cultural pluralism without hierarchy.

■ ■ ■

EUGENE D. GENOVESE

■ ■ ■

WHO WANTS to be accused of insensitivity? The answer is, Those who recognize "sensitivity" as a code word for the promulgation of a demagogic political program. At Brooklyn College, which I attended in the late 1940s, everyone took for granted that students ought to challenge their professors and one another. Professors acted as if they were paid to assault their students' sensibilities, to offend their most cherished values. The classroom was an ideological war zone. And self-respecting students returned the blows. In this way we had a chance to acquire a first-rate education, that is, to learn to sustain ourselves in combat against dedicated but overworked professors who lacked the time and the "tolerance" to worry about our "feelings."

I learned my lessons well, and so I routinely assign books that contradict the point of view presented in my own classroom. I insist only that students challenge my point of view in accordance with the canons of (Southern) courtesy, and in obedience to a rule: Lay down plausible premises, argue logically, appeal to evidence. If they say things that offend others, the offended ones are invited to reply, fiercely but in accordance with the same courtesy and in obedience to the same rule. I know no other way to show students, white or black, male or female, the respect that ought to be shown in a place of intellectual and ideological contention. Thus I submit the First Law of College Teaching: *Any professor who, subject to the restraints of common sense and common decency, does not seize every opportunity to offend the sensibilities of his students is insulting and cheating them, and is no college professor at all.*

■ ■ ■

ELIZABETH FOX-GENOVESE

■ ■ ■

FEW WOULD CONTEST the obvious truth that we live in a multicultural world and that the more we know about it, the more productive citizens we are likely to be. But in most instances, the defense of multiculturalism does not propose to prepare us with any rigor to be citizens of that world. It does not, for instance, usually take the form of impassioned requests for more and stiffer language requirements. Rarely does it take the form of demands for greater exposure to the elite texts of other cultures. Even more rarely does it take the form of pleas for substantive training in economics or geography. Clearly, multiculturalism in its most pervasive form is not viewed as a skill. Multiculturalism primarily consists in exposure to English language texts that testify to and affirm the diversity of the personal experience of those who have reason to believe that their kind has been oppressed and excluded by dead white men.

At the core of the multicultural agenda lies a commitment to education—and, indeed, culture itself—as primarily the quest for an acceptable autobiography. Multiculturalists, building upon the demands for "relevance," assume that education must, above all, strengthen the student's positive sense of identity. Racial and ethnic pride, in this perspective, serve to strengthen individual self-confidence. Multiculturalism of this kind does not even, or necessarily, promote toleration for the diversity of others. If members of different racial and ethnic groups may unite in an initial demand for multicultural education, they may also rapidly divide over the respective claims of different ethnicities on the assumption that no one who is not of one's own kind can understand one's specific experience.

In real terms, however, the battle over multiculturalism is a battle over scarce resources and shrinking opportunities. To recognize this much does not deny the related battle over national identity, but does caution us to take the more extreme pronouncements pro and con with a grain of salt.

■ ■ ■

MICHELE WALLACE

■ ■ ■

I CONSIDER multiculturalism to be a bourgeois, academic phenomenon. It would have to be. For the most part, anything originating from a white perspective that uses the same kind of knowledge to look at Afro-Americans as well as Koreans or Puerto Ricans in his country, without an acknowledgement of class, gender, how long they have been here, whether their immigration was illegal or legal, I have to call profoundly antihistorical and antimaterialist and probably racist to boot. I'm not opposed to theorizing multiculturalism. [But] it can only be useful if it is an opportunity to theorize the multiple theoretical positions of minorities in First World countries and the problems of Third World peoples in Third World countries. . . . There is always a need to ask economic and material questions of one's multicultural ideas.

■ ■ ■

LOUIS MENAND

■ ■ ■

ACADEMIC ACTIVISTS may think otherwise, but conservatives like D'Souza would love to debate curriculum reform with them forever, because changing the curriculum is the cheapest social program ever devised.

■ ■ ■

CORNEL WEST

■ ■ ■

THE POLITICAL CHALLENGE is to articulate universality in a way that is not a mere smoke screen for someone else's particularity. We must preserve the possibility of universal connection. That's the fundamental challenge. Let's dig deep enough within our heritage to make that connection to others.

We're not naive, we know that argument and critical exchange are not the major means by which social change takes place in the world. But we recognize that they have to have a role, have to have a function. Therefore, we will trash older notions of objectivity and not act as if one group or community or one nation has a god's-

-eye view of the world. Instead we will utilize forms of intersub-
jectivity that facilitate critical exchange even as we recognize that
none of us are free of presuppositions and prejudgments. We will
put our arguments on the table and allow them to be interrogated
and contested. The quest for knowledge without presuppositions,
the quest for certainty, the quest for dogmatism and orthodoxy
and rigidity is over.

■ ■ ■

ELEANOR HEARTNEY

■ ■ ■

POSSIBLY THE GREATEST danger currently facing
American society is the decay of the public sphere and the
disintegration of the public interest into an atomized collection of
narrow, localized, and often ethnically defined special interests.
The social chaos and pointless destruction that result from such
Balkanization is only too obvious elsewhere in the world – in the
bloody clashes between Sikhs and Hindus, Slovenes, Croats, and
Serbs, Romanians and Hungarians, the African National Party
and the Zulus, and, last but not least, the Baltic states and the Soviet Union.

In an article on the decline of democracy in America, Lewis
Lapham described the ideal from which we have so egregiously
fallen: "Democratic government is a purpose held in common,
and if it can be understood as a field of temporary coalitions
among people of different interests, skills, and generations, then
everybody has need of everybody else." Militant multiculturalism
rejects this ideal, scornfully dismissing visions of a more egalitarian society capable of addressing and reconciling the conflicting
needs and desires of its various constituencies in a peaceable

fashion as naive and utopian. But the alternative to the liberal dream would seem to be an ever more divided society where charges and countercharges drown out the few embattled voices calling for a search for common ground. Unless we find some way to pass messages across cultural and racial battle lines, we seem likely to bury ourselves beneath the ruins of our own Tower of Babel. With the common projects of social justice and preservation of freedom cast into disarray by the confusion of tongues, we will be lost in fruitless combat with adversaries who ought to be our friends.

■ ■ ■

MICHAEL BÉRUBÉ

■ ■ ■

I MYSELF AM the product of more core curricula than most of you will ever want to see. Throughout my undergraduate years, I never once heard Zora Neale Hurston's name — or Mary Wollstonecraft's, or Aphra Behn's. Even as an English major specializing in American literature, I was assigned one book by a black writer — American literature's number one crossover hit, *The Invisible Man*. That was nearly ten years ago, and it's safe to say that it wouldn't happen quite that way today. But who knows? I was assigned to read a book by a writer of African descent only in my fourteenth of fourteen graduate courses at Virginia, when the English department managed to hire someone who could teach courses in which "American" was not automatically synonymous with "white."

In that fourteenth graduate course (on the modern American long poem), I came across Melvin Tolson, whose 170-page *Harlem Gallery*, published in 1965, is one of those neglected masterpieces that's fallen out of print and out of whatever passes for our cultural memory. It's Tolson who reminds me now that the canon revisions of the past fifteen years have not attacked Western culture; they have, above all, *enriched* our sense of Western culture. But precisely because we've done so much to recover some of the West's suppressed heterogeneities, we cannot stand mutely by while the West is defended by a phalanx of conservative journalists and political hacks who apparently read only one another. Under normal circumstances, it would be bad enough that the academy's attackers have so little understanding of what they're attacking; but what's truly scandalous about these people is that they so often have just as little understanding of what they're defending. If the legacy of Western culture is to be entrusted to the likes of Kimball, Taylor, D'Souza, and the scribes at *Newsweek*, then we can be sure that it will not truly be a legacy of "Western culture" – and it will not be a legacy worthy preserving.

CONTRIBUTORS

MORTIMER J. ADLER is the author of 44 books, the editor of *Great Books of the Western World*, the chairman of the board of editors of the *Encyclopaedia Britannica*, and the director of the Institute for Philosophical Research.

MOLEFI KETE ASANTE is the chairman of the African-American Studies department at Temple University, the editor of the *Journal of Black Studies*, and the author of many books, including *Kemet, Afrocentricity and Knowledge*.

PATRICIA AUFDERHEIDE is an assistant professor in the School of Communication at The American University and a senior editor of *In These Times* newspaper. She is an associate editor of *Black Film Review* and has published widely in newspapers and magazines.

KATHARINE T. BARTLETT is a professor of law at Duke University.

DAVID BEERS is a senior editor of *Mother Jones*.

PAULA BENNETT is a professor in the English department at Southern Illinois University.

MICHAEL BÉRUBÉ is an assistant professor at the University of Illinois at Urbana-Champagne, where he holds appointments in the Department of English and Unit for Criticism and Interpretive Theory.

HARRY C. BOYTE is a senior fellow and director of Project Public Life at the Hubert H. Humphrey Institute of Public Affairs of the University of Minnesota, and the author of *Common Wealth: A Return to Citizen Politics*.

LINDA BRODKEY is the director of lower division English at the University of Texas at Austin, and the author of *Academic Writing as Social Practice*.

REED WAY DASENBROCK is a professor of English at New Mexico State University, Las Cruces.

SARA DIAMOND is the author of *Spiritual Warfare: The Politics of the Christian Right*, and currently a Ph.D. candidate at the University of California at Berkeley, where she is writing a sociological history of U.S. right-wing movement.

DINESH D'SOUZA is currently a research fellow at the American Enterprise Institute in Washington, D.C., and the author of *Illiberal Education: The Politics of Race and Sex on Campus*.

MARTIN DUBERMAN is the Distinguished Professor of History at the Graduate Center of the City University of New York, and the founder of the Center for Gay and Lesbian Studies; his books include a biography of Paul Robeson and a memoir entitled *Cures*.

TROY DUSTER is a professor of sociology at the University of California at Berkeley.

ROSA EHRENREICH is a graduate of Harvard University, and currently a Marshall Scholar at Oxford University.

BARBARA EPSTEIN is a professor of history at the University of California at Santa Cruz.

SARA M. EVANS is a professor of history at the University of Minnesota, and the author of *Born for Liberty: A History of Women in America*.

SHELLI FOWLER is a Ph.D. student in the English department at the University of Texas at Austin.

ELIZABETH FOX-GENOVESE is the director of Women's Studies and the Eleonore Raoul Professor of History at Emory University, and the author of *Within the Plantation Household: Black and White Women of the Old South*, and *Feminism Without Illusions: A Critique of Individualism*.

EUGENE D. GENOVESE is the Distinguished Scholar-in-Residence at The University Center in Georgia, and the author of *The Slaveholders' Dilemma: Freedom and Progress in Southern Conservative Thought, 1820–1860*.

TODD GITLIN is a professor of sociology at the University of California at Berkeley, and the author of *The Sixties: Years of Hope, Days of Rage*.

MILES HARVEY is co–managing editor of *In These Times*.

ELEANOR HEARTNEY is a contributing editor of *New Art Examiner*, and writes for various publications, including *Art in America* and *Artnews*.

NAT HENTOFF is a columnist at the *Village Voice* and the *Washington Post*, and a staff writer at the *New Yorker*.

NINA KING is the editor of the *Washington Post Book World*.

LOUIS MENAND teaches English at Queens College and at the Graduate Center of the City of New York, and was a Guggenheim Fellow in 1991.

RAOUL V. MOWATT is a senior English major at Stanford, and the former managing editor of the *Stanford Daily*.

RUTH PERRY teaches at the Program in Women's Studies at the Massachusetts Institute of Technology.

DIANE RAVITCH is the Assistant United States Secretary of Education, and the author of *The Troubled Crusade: American Education, 1945–1980*.

JOAN WALLACH SCOTT is a professor of social science at the Institute for Advanced Study, Princeton, New Jersey, and the author of *Gender and the Politics of History*.

MICHELE WALLACE teaches literature at the City College of New York, and is the author of *Black Macho and the Myth of the Superwoman*.

JACOB WEISBERG is a senior editor at the *New Republic*.

CORNEL WEST is DSA honorary chair, the director of Afro-American Studies at Princeton, and the author of *The Ethical Dimensions of Marxism*.

JON WIENER teaches American history at the University of California at Irvine, and is a contributing editor of the *Nation*.

ROGER WILKINS is a journalist and fellow at the Institute for Policy Studies.

GEORGE F. WILL is a nationally syndicated columnist, and a former professor of political philosophy.

PATRICIA J. WILLIAMS is a professor of law at the University of Wisconsin, and the author of *The Alchemy of Race and Rights*.

SHAWN WONG is a professor of American Ethnic Studies at the University of Washington, the editor of four anthologies on Asian American literature, and the author of a novel entitled *Homophobe*.

C. VANN WOODWARD is the Sterling Professor of History Emeritus at Yale, and the author of *The Old World's New World*.

This book is
set in Bodoni Book,
type by The Typeworks
and manufactured by
Edwards Brothers, Inc.
on acid-free paper.